THE INFLUENCE OF NATURAL RELIGION *ON THE* TEMPORAL HAPPINESS OF MANKIND

Titles on the Philosophy of Religion in Prometheus's Great Books in Philosophy Series

Jeremy Bentham .... *The Influence of Natural Religion on the Temporal Happiness of Mankind*

Marcus Tullius Cicero .... *The Nature of the Gods* and *On Divination*

Ludwig Feuerbach .... *The Essence of Christianity*

David Hume .... *Dialogues Concerning Natural Religion*

John Locke .... *A Letter Concerning Toleration*

Lucretius .... *On the Nature of Things*

John Stuart Mill .... *Three Essays on Religion*

Friedrich Nietzsche .... *The Antichrist*

Thomas Paine .... *The Age of Reason*

Bertrand Russell .... *Bertrand Russell on God and Religion*

See the back of this volume for a complete list of titles in Prometheus's Great Books in Philosophy Series.

THE INFLUENCE OF NATURAL RELIGION *ON THE* TEMPORAL HAPPINESS OF MANKIND

Introduction by Delos McKown

JEREMY
BENTHAM

GREAT BOOKS IN PHILOSOPHY

59 John Glenn Drive
Amherst, New York 14228-2197

Published 2003 by Prometheus Books
59 John Glenn Drive, Amherst, New York 14228–2197.
VOICE: 716–691–0133, ext. 207. FAX: 716–564–2711.
WWW.PROMETHEUSBOOKS.COM

Library of Congress Cataloging-in-Publication Data

Beauchamp, Philip.
[Analysis of the influence of natural religion on the temporal happiness of mankind]
The influence of natural religion on the temporal happiness of mankind / Jeremy Bentham ; introduction by Delos McKown.
p. cm. (Great books in philosophy)
Originally published: Analysis of the influence of natural religion on the temporal happiness of mankind. London : R. Carlile, 1822. With new introd.
Includes bibliographical references.
ISBN 1–59102–033–6 (alk. paper)
1. Natural theology. I. Bentham, Jeremy, 1748–1832. II. Title. III. Series.

BL183 .B43 2002
210—dc21 2002031851

Printed in the United States of America on acid-free paper

JEREMY BENTHAM, was born in London on February 15, 1748, to a family of comfortable means. His was the life of a child prodigy who read Latin at three years of age and at twelve was enrolled in Oxford university, where he received his undergraduate degree at the age of sixteen. Thereafter, he studied law at Lincoln's Inn, Westminster. Inheritances from his parents afforded Bentham the opportunity to pursue a life of study and writing. While in his mid-forties, he dedicated himself to the critical analysis and reform of moral, political, religious, legal, education, and economic institutions.

Though he found the judicial system to be hypocritical and corrupt, Bentham's fascination with the fundamental ideals of the law steered him twoard philosophy and science in an effort to develop standards that could ground the social order. His reformist tendencies proved to be a significant factor in the development of his now famous system of ethics known as utilitarianism, wherein human action was to be judged by the amount of pleasure and pain it produced.

Bentham's published works include: *A Fragment on Government* (1776), *An Introduction to the Principles of Morals and Legislation* (1781), *Analysis of the Influence of Natural Religion on the Temporal Happiness of Mankind* (1822), *The Rationale of Judicial Evidence* (edited by John Stuart Mill in 1825), and two volumes on *Constitutional Code* (ca. 1830). Bentham died in London on June 16, 1832.

Introduction

In 1822 there was published in London, England, a slender but singular volume entitled *Analysis of the Influence of Natural Religion on the Temporal Happiness of Mankind.* It bore the name of a certain Philip Beauchamp. The very title of this work requires explication. Natural religion herein is to be understood as religion stemming from rational theology alone. Its antithesis is not unnatural religion, as though there were any such species of faith, but, rather, revealed religion. The *Analysis* is totally uninterested in whether or not there is any one or other objectively revealed religion. It is satisfied to recognize as revealed any religion whose adherents claim that it is revealed. Thus, it avoids any epistemological concern. Its professed concern, rather, is with the emotional and physical implications of rational theology as these bear upon the temporal happiness of those who espouse it.

To examine rational religion with an eye to earthly and/or temporal happiness is to set it at odds with Christianity—the dominant *revealed* religion of the West. Christianity is primarily concerned not with earthly and/or temporal happiness in terrestrial life but with unearthly and/or timeless happiness in an eternal celestial realm, presumably entered (by the redeemed) upon dying. This temporal world (in bondage to Satan and other malign agents) is a place where Christians must bear their crosses, expecting persecution (Matt. 10:16–23), suffering family strife (Luke 12:51–53, 21:16–17), and submitting themselves to governing authorities as established by the Bible-god (Rom. 13:1–7, Titus 3:1, 1 Peter 2:13–14). Neither Christian Lords Spiritual nor Lords Temporal were much concerned about how Christianity might conduce in the present to the personal happiness of their slaves, servants, serfs, vassals, or assorted underlings. It was enough that those in the lower orders should do their duty to their betters and stand ready, as sheep, to be shorn, sacrificed, or slaughtered as needed.

It was bad enough for literate English Christians, of whatever stripe, to be confronted by a book that ignored the presumed truths of their revealed religion in favor of natural (or rational) religion; even worse to be confronted by a book that took a Utilitarian position respecting the relation of natural religion to the personal, temporal happiness or unhappiness of those who believed therein. In short, it left open the unheard-of possibility that a religion that led to more unhappiness than happiness in this life might better be ignored.

Despite being calumniated for being atheistic, the *Analysis* never denies that the cosmos might be (or is) artifactual. Thus, it never denies that there might have been (or may still be) a cosmic artificer. Moreover, in its definition of religion, it is content to accept the idea that this inferential entity might be almighty. Finally, in the same definition, it accepts the notion that human souls might live after death to reap eternal weal or suffer endless woe. Only theists, made reckless by their detestation of the *Analysis*, could accuse it of atheism. The garden variety of English deists had also been (and were still being) accused of atheism by various ignorant enemies. Up to this point, then, the *Analysis* appears to be just another more or less offensive volume in the deistic tradition. The radical turn it takes from traditional deism lies in the conclusions it draws concerning the character of the divine (albeit inferential) entity and in what this implies for deistic faith in a providential order. Readers are best left to themselves to discover (in the text that follows) the *empirical* reasons given for these surprising departures.

The *Analysis* is divided into two parts. The first part generally maintains its focus on natural religion, i.e., on bare-bones theism as opposed to the theologically embroidered theisms one finds in such "revealed" religions as Judaism, Christianity, or Islam. The second section either loses this focus unintentionally or, as some critics have maintained, refocuses on its real target—Christianity. Although the author never mentions Christianity, it is clear that he has organized religion in mind. It is equally clear, historically, that the dominant organized religion of his time and place was Christianity. Among the evils of (organized) religion listed by the author is its standing army of priests, an army neither needed nor possessed by natural religionists, but an army both needed and possessed by state churches such as the Anglican Church in England and the Catholic Church in countries elsewhere in Europe. Paramount among the evils attributable to this army is the mental depravity it creates in people, particularly in helpless children. In this connection, the *Analysis* contains a provocative characterization of insanity, to wit: Insanity occurs when the beliefs people entertain are totally divorced from their empirically based experiences. It should be obvious to all that the feigned objects of religious faith, zealously inculcated by the clergy, are devoid of empirical foundations.

The question now arises, who was this Philip Beachamp that he should so deftly have torpedoed deism (the thoughtful person's religion) and so trenchantly have skewered "revealed," organized, depraved religion—in one fell swoop? Was he (a) a reclusive English aristocrat scribbling his audacious thoughts in England's bosky countryside, (b) a mordant don having theological axes to grind while lecturing at Oxford or Cambridge, (c) an embittered priest secretly attacking religion while teaching divinity at some religious institute or other, or (d) none of the above? The answer is "d," for "Philip Beauchamp" was merely a pseudonym, a pseudonym for a certain George Grote. But who, pray, was he, and why did he feel the need for a pseudonym?

George Grote (1794–1871) was an Englishman of many parts. As a young man he was a banker and businessman, and even when he was no longer active in banking, his financial acumen was called upon over and again. By training, he was a classical scholar, a published historian of Greece, a philologist, and an author of works on Plato and Aristotle. He was also a political scientist, a (somewhat reluctant) member of Parliament briefly, and always a reformer, having been active (as a nonpolitician) prior to 1832 on behalf of the famous Reform Bill of that year. As an educator he was a founding father of the secular institution that was to evolve into the University of London and for a time a senior administrator of it during a phase in its early development. Why should such a person have written such a work as the *Analysis*? To answer this, we must look behind George Grote much as we had earlier to look behind Philip Beauchamp. Upon doing this, we come upon none other than Jeremy Bentham, the major developer, if not the sole founder, of Utilitarian moral philosophy, a totally secular moral philosophy that he was prepared to set, with gusto, against all the religiously sanctioned moral systems of the world.

Today, Jeremy Bentham (1748–1832) is both well known and scarcely known at all. He is best known to professional philosophers and students of ethics for his consequentialist moral philosophy, called Utilitarianism; simultaneously he is known as a mentor of John Stuart Mill, who eclipsed him philosophically. He is known to students of jurisprudence, whether in law school or not, as an archenemy of the pontifical Blackstone. He is known to academic penologists and to the more learned variety of prison wardens as a would-be penal reformer. He is known to political theorists as a writer of constitutions and law codes and as a derider of the twin notions of natural law and natural rights. He is known to the more historically minded of psychologists for his associationism and behaviorism. He is known to students of the philosophy of language and to historians of logic for his theory of fictions. But, and this is significant, he is known to theologians not at all. Learned divines would find themselves in professional peril were they to venture into his devastating analyses of their aëriel science.

Bentham calls to mind Jesus' claim that prophets are not without honor except in their own land and among their own people. He was, for example, more respected in France (and perhaps better known) than in England. This may be due in part to his style of life. He was so comfortable financially that he did not have to earn his daily bread; so disdainful of British higher education that he never sought an academic forum for his ideas; so lacking in literary vanity that he did not care who disseminated his ideas; and so indifferent to popularity that he was content to live reclusively. He did, however, attract disciples, among whom was George Grote. Grote had come to know James Mill (John Stuart Mill's father) in 1818 and through him, in 1820, to meet Bentham and to fall under his influence.

As early as 1815, Bentham had begun to assemble his jottings on the subject matter that was eventually to find its way into the *Analysis*. Although he wrote voluminously throughout his adult life on a wide range of topics, his writing was not primarily for publication but for the clarification of his own thoughts concerning whatever piqued his curiosity at any given moment. Not needing to publish, either for fame or fortune, and, hence, not having to meet editors' deadlines, he was free to drop a writing project at any time whenever he noticed something new holding greater, if only temporary, enticements. Thus, he left behind stacks of paper, disorganized, unfinished, and unpublished. One such stack he conveyed to Grote with leave to organize its contents for publication.

Disputes have arisen among scholars as to how much of the

Analysis was contributed by Bentham, how much by Grote. Opinions have run the gamut from seeing Bentham as the major contributor, Grote the minor, to seeing Grote as the major contributor, Bentham the minor. One point is clear: Bentham did not write the *Analysis* in its present form, for it is a finished, graceful piece of prose, readily accessible to the reader. Bentham's writing, on the contrary, was most often crabbed, turgid, or frightfully daunting. Forgetting style for a time and focusing on content instead, those who view Grote as the major contributor, Bentham the minor, will have to explain why there is nothing surprising, discordant, or inconsistent in the *Analysis* when its contents are set alongside of Bentham's other (often scattered) writings on religion.

It is easy to develop a list of comparisons between the two. In both one finds (1) pervasive Utilitarianism, (2) hostility to all religiously based ethics, (3) similar definitions of religion, (4) willingness to accept the idea of a Supreme Being as a permissible inference, (5) a loathing of oaths (especially when coerced), (6) ridicule of natural rights and of natural law (when such law is applied to human behavior rather than to the natural world), (7) a sociomorphic view of the Deity of natural religion as modeled on earthly sovereigns, (8) detestation of the routine mendacity of the clergy, (9) revulsion at their role in depraving the minds of children (through the inanity of catechetical instruction), and (10) a recognition of the unholy alliance between the Crown and the Altar in exploiting all others, taken respectively to be mere subjects or sheep. This list could be extended, but to do so would be to carry coals to Newcastle.

However, one crucial strand of Bentham's thought, which is to be found running throughout his writings on language, logic, and ontology, is missing from the *Analysis*. I have already hinted at it when using the abstract terms the *Crown* and the *Altar*. The crucial strand at issue is Bentham's philosophy of language, especially his theory of fictions. In short, to him all nouns naming abstractions name fictitious entities. To confuse these verbally with the names of real entities, whether physical or psychical, is to fall into endless confusion. Although this strand of his thought could have been woven into the *Analysis*, there was never any necessity for doing so. Hence, its absence therein may not be telling. In view of the foregoing, I think we are safe in concluding that the *Analysis* exhibits the clear and trenchant mind of Bentham on religion in the discerning and graceful hand of Grote.

If one approaches the *Analysis* ontologically, i.e., in terms of that which has being and that (so to speak) which does not, then it is not an atheistic work, as noted earlier. It never denies that the cosmos might be artifactual, that it might, thus, be the work of a Divine Artificer. It accepts the deistic presumption as a permissible inference. Similarly, if one approaches the *Analysis* epistemologically, i.e., in terms of what can be known and what cannot be known, then it is not an atheistic work either. It never asserts that the cosmos can be known to be natural and, thus, not artifactual. But, if one equates atheism with godlessness, then by inference the *Analysis* is atheistic, for its authors were godless. Neither Bentham nor Grote inferred a Cosmic Artificer, neither suffered the intuition that he was the object of divine espionage; neither worshipped anything, and neither, as an adult, predicated any of his moral decisions on the positive and/or negative sanctions of a Cosmic Artificer. To equate godlessness with atheism, however, is to commit a logical blunder. Godlessness is a characteristic of certain individual human beings. It is a biographical fact, so to speak, having nothing to do with ontology on a cosmic scale. In short, one can be godless in daily life without denying the deistic presumption.

The monarchs of England and the archbishops of the Anglican Church did not care to entertain such nice distinctions between atheism and godlessness as I have just made. Moreover, these royal and reverend personages could find ways to restrict, if not silence, such miscreants as known atheists, openly godless folk, and even avowed deists. Through the unholy alliance between the Crown and the Altar, voluble unbelievers, of whatever stripe, could be arrested, tried, and punished on such trumped-up charges as blasphemy, libel, or slander—in varying combinations. To underscore this point, Richard Carlile, the radical freethinker who published the *Analysis*, was caged in Dorchester prison at the time of its publication. Bentham, even before becoming the self-conscious founder of Utilitarian moral philosophy, knew well how to balance the pleasures of freedom against the pains of incarceration. He was, accordingly, as circumspect as possible, actively fearing whatever retribution the authorities might wreak upon him, especially when still young and not as famous as he was to become in old age. Similarly, George Grote, who at the time stood on the brink of a brilliant academic career and who had no stomach just then for risking his future, experienced more than a little trepidation for his part in producing the *Analysis*. Thus was trundled on stage the non–deus (*sic*) ex machina of Philip Beauchamp.

The *Analysis* died aborning and was buried in an unmarked grave. It died aborning in that scarcely anyone read it. The few who did preferred to damn it as a trifling tract, not worthy of philosophically respectable attempts at refutation. Since it was profoundly disquieting to theologians, whether in the natural or in the revealed camp, it was thought better to belittle it than to risk being bested by it. Its burial in an unmarked grave, so to speak, requires at bit of explanation. It was Benjamin Franklin, if memory serves me aright, who said something to the effect that it is an unwise man who chooses his physician as his heir. This can be paraphrased to say that it is an unwise writer of godless literature who chooses a pious believer (even if a Unitarian) as his literary executor. Yet, this is what Bentham did in choosing John Bowring who, in assembling and editing the *Works of Jeremy Bentham* (in eleven volumes), simply left most of Bentham's writings on religion out. These were, after all, to Bowring too "bold and adventurous for publication." Not even John Stuart Mill's praise of the *Analysis* could save it from oblivion.

We who are Christian in culture, if not in creed, know as well as do faithful Christians that something momentous follows death and burial—yes, resurrection! It is my hope that the interest of Prometheus Books in reprinting the *Analysis* and in including it in its Great Books in Philosophy Series will lead to a marvelous, if not a miraculous, resurrection. The *Analysis of the Influence of Natural Religion on the Temporal Happiness of Mankind* does not deserve the oblivion to which it has, hitherto, been consigned.

Delos B. McKown
Professor Emeritus of Philosophy
Auburn University

Analysis of the Influence of Natural Religion on the Temporal Happiness of Mankind

BY PHILIP BEAUCHAMP

Preface

The following pages present a temperate, and I hope a satisfactory, examination of the temporal good or evil produced by Natural Religion. The topic is of unspeakable importance, and has by no means met with the attention which it deserves. It has indeed scarcely ever been separately considered, and those who have controverted the truth of religion have suffered themselves with but little opposition to be decried as inflicting the deepest injury upon humanity—as corrupting the most effectual source both of rectitude and of consolation—and as robbing mankind of doctrines, which, supposing they were false, ought nevertheless to have been invented and inculcated. Such has been the current opinion on the subject: and it need not be remarked how strong must have been the inclination of an audience so prepossessed, to support that which they regarded as the firmest tie and protection of society.

It is therefore essentially requisite, before the question as to the truth of religion can be brought to a fair and unbiassed decision, to estimate correctly the advantages or disadvantages which result from its adoption. If the estimate of these advantages drawn up by its advocates be really well-founded, we may safely pronounce that no anti-religious writer could possibly make a convert, even though he were armed with demonstration as rigorous as that of Euclid.

Should the following reasonings be deemed conclusive, a clear idea may be formed of the temporal gain or loss accruing from the agency of Natural Religion. Whether the doctrines which this term involves be true or false, is a point on which I do not intend to touch: nor is the question of any import, so far as regards the present discussion. Though these doctrines were false, yet many religionists allege that it would be salutary to deceive mankind into a belief of their truth: And conversely, others might with equal right maintain, that although they were true, it might perhaps still be pernicious, so far as regards the present life, to receive them as true.

Under the term *Natural Religion*, I include all religious belief not specially determined and settled by some revelation (or reputed revelation) from the Being to whom the belief relates. The good or bad temporal tendency of any particular alleged revelation, can of course only be ascertained by an inspection of the books in which it is contained, and must therefore form a separate enquiry. To any such enquiry however, the present discussion is an essential preliminary. For if it be discovered that Religion, unassisted by revelation, is the foe and not the benefactor of mankind, we can then ascertain whether the good effects engrafted upon her by any alleged revelation, are sufficient to neutralise the bitterness of her natural fruits. Nor is it possible to measure the benefit or injury derived from revealed Religion, without first determining the effects of Religion herself without any revelation.

Divines have on many occasions admitted and enlarged upon the defects and bad tendency of Natural Religion. Hence, they infer, the necessity of a revelation. Whoever contends that a revelation was a present highly necessary, and a most signal instance of the benevolence of God; must also contend that the pre-existing religion was, to say the least, productive of a very slender portion of good. And if our present enquiry should demonstrate that Natural Religion has produced a large balance of temporal evil above temporal good, this will evince still more forcibly the necessity of a revelation such as to purge and counteract its bad effects.

To obviate all misconceptions, I wish to declare beforehand, that whenever the general term *religion* is used in the following treatise I mean it to denote *mere Natural* Religion, apart from Revelation. If I do not constantly annex the qualifying epithet *natural*, it is from a wish to avoid needless repetition of that which may be indicated once for all in the beginning. In the same manner I wish it to be understood, that whenever the terms, *sacerdotal class*, or any synonymous phrases, are employed, it is only the ministers of Natural Religion who are designated.

Table of Contents

PART I

CHAPTER I

Preliminary statements and definition.

On the truth of religion much has been urged; on its usefulness and beneficial tendency, comparatively little—little, at least, which can be termed argumentative or convincing. But assumption is shorter than proof, and the advocates of religion, though scarcely deigning to bestow any inquiry or analysis upon the subject, have not failed to ascribe to it results of supreme excellence and happiness. It has been affirmed to be the leading bond of union between the different members of society—to be the most powerful curb on the immoral and unsocial passions of individuals—to form the consolation and support of misfortunes and declining life—in short it has been described as the most efficient prop both of inward happiness and of virtuous practice in this world. Whether these sublime pretensions are well-founded or not, the following inquiry is destined to ascertain.

The warmest partisan of natural religion cannot deny, that by the influence of it (occasionally at least) bad effects have been produced; nor can any one on the other hand venture to deny, that it has on other occasions brought about good effects. The question therefore is, throughout, only as to the comparative magnitude, number, and proportion of each.

One course has indeed been adopted, by means of which religion has been, in appearance, extricated from all imputation, of having ever given birth to ill effects in any shape. So far as the results occasioned by it have been considered as good, the producing cause has been termed *religion*. So far as these results have been regarded as bad, this name has been discarded and the word *superstition* has been substituted. Or these injurious effects have avowedly been thrown aside under the pretence, that they are *abuses of religion*; that the abuse of a thing cannot be urged against its use, since the most beneficent preparations may be erroneously or criminally applied. By these false methods of reasoning the subject has been inconceivably overclouded, and it is therefore essentially necessary to expose and guard against such fallacies in the outset. From the former of these two sources all deception will be obviated by an accurate definition of the term *religion*; by strictly confining it to one meaning, and invariably introducing it whenever that meaning is implied. Against the latter principle, by which what are called the abuses of a thing are discarded from the estimate of its real importance and value, we declare open war. By the use of a thing, is meant the good which it produces; by the abuse, the evil which it occasions. To pronounce upon the merits of the thing under discussion, previously erasing from the reckoning all the evil which it occasions, is most preposterous and unwarrantable. Were this mode of summing up receipts and eluding all deduction of outgoings, admissible, every institution, which had ever produced any good effects at all, must be applauded as meritorious and useful, although its pernicious effects, which had been thrust out of the account, might form a decided and overwhelming balance on the other side.

By the term *religion* is meant the belief in the existence of an almighty Being, by whom pains and pleasures will be dispensed to mankind, during an infinite and future state of existence. And religion is called natural, when there exists no written and acknowledged declaration, from which an acquaintance with the will and attributes of this almighty Being may be gathered.

My object is therefore to ascertain, whether the belief of posthumous pains and pleasures, then to be administered by an omnipotent Being, is useful to mankind—that is, productive of happiness or misery in the present life.

I say, *in the present life*, for the distinction is exceedingly important to notice. Compared with an interminable futurity, the present life taken in its almost duration, is but as a point, less than a drop of water to the ocean. Although, therefore, it should be demonstrated, that religion, considered with reference to the present life, is not beneficial but pernicious—not *augmentative* but destructive of human happiness—there might still remain ample motive to the observance of its precepts, in the mind of a true believer.

CHAPTER II

The Expectations of posthumous Pain and Pleasure, which Natural Religion holds out, considered simply and in themselves.

The pains and pleasures, which are believed to await us in a posthumous existence, may be anticipated either as conditional, and dependent upon the present behaviour of the believer, or as unconditional dispensations, which no conduct on his part can either amend or aggravate. Though perhaps it is impossible to produce any case in which the belief has actually assumed this latter shape, yet it will be expedient to survey it in this most general and indeterminate form, before we introduce the particular circumstances which have usually accompanied the reception of it. A few considerations will suffice to ascertain, whether expectations of posthumous pains and pleasures, considered in themselves and without any reference to the direction which they may give to human conduct, are of a nature to occasion happiness or misery to the believer.

Nothing can be more undeniable, than that a posthumous existence, if sincerely anticipated, is most likely to appear replete with impending pain and misery. The demonstration is brief and decisive.

A posthumous state of existence is necessarily unknown and

impervious to human vision. We cannot see the ground which is before us; We possess not the slightest means of knowing whether it resembles that which we have already trodden. The scene before us is wrapped in impenetrable darkness. In this state of obscurity and ignorance, the imagination usurps the privilege of filling up the void, and what are the scenes which she pourtrays? They are similar to those with which the mind is overrun during a state of earthly darkness—the product of unmixed timidity and depression. Fear is the never-failing companion and offspring of ignorance, and the circumstances of human life infallibly give birth to such a communion. For the painful sensations are the most obtrusive and constant assailants which lie in ambush round our path. The first years of our life are spent in suffering under their sting, before we acquire the means of warding them off. The sole acquisition applicable to this purpose is knowledge—knowledge of the precise manner and occasion in which we are threatened, and of the antidote which may obviate it. Still however the painful sensations are continually on the watch to take advantage of every unguarded moment; nor is there a single hour of our life in which the lessons of experience are not indispensibly necessary for our protection against them.

Since then it is only to knowledge that we owe our respite from perpetual suffering; wherever our knowledge fails us and we are reduced to a state of unprotected helplessness, all our sense of security, all anticipations of future ease, must vanish along with it. Ignorance must generate incessant alarm and uneasiness. The regular economy of the universe, by which nature is subjected to general laws, and the past becomes the interpreter of the future, is often adduced as a reason for extolling the beneficence of the Deity; and a reliance on the stability of *events*, as well as in the efficacy of the provision we have made against the future, is justly regarded as the most indispensible ingredient in human happiness. Had we no longer any confident expectation that to-morrow would resemble yesterday—were we altogether without any rule for predicting what would occur to us after this night, how shocking would be our alarm and depression? The unknown future, which was about to succeed, would be pregnant to our affrighted imaginations, with calamity from which we knew not how to shelter ourselves. Infants are timorous to a proverb, and perhaps there is scarcely any man, possessed of vision, whom darkness does not impress with some degree of apprehension and uneasiness. Yet if a man fancies himself unsheltered, when only the visible prognostics of impending evil are effaced, while all his other means of foresight and defence remain inviolate, how much keener will be the sense of his unprotected condition, when all means of predicting or averting future calamity are removed beyond his reach? If, in the one case, his alarmed fancy peoples the darkness with unreal enemies, and that too in defiance of the opposing assurances of reason, what an array of suffering will it conjure up in the other, where the ignorance and helplessness, upon which the alarm is founded, is so infinitely magnified, and where reason cannot oppose the smallest tittle of evidence?

I have thus endeavoured to show that from the unintermitting peril to which human life is exposed, and the perpetual necessity of knowledge to protect ourselves against it, mankind must infallibly conceive an unknown future as fraught with misery and torment. But this is not the only reason which may be assigned for such a tendency. Pain is a far stronger, more pungent, and more distinct sensation than pleasure; it is more various in its shapes, more definite and impressive upon the memory, and lays hold of the imagination with greater mastery and permanence. Pain, therefore, is far more likely to obtrude itself upon the conceptions, where there exists no positive evidence to circumscribe their range, than pleasure. Throughout the catalogue of human suspicions, there exists not a case in which our ignorance is so profound as about the manner of a posthumous existence; and since no reason can be given for preferring one mode of conceiving it to another, the strongest sensations of the past will be perfectly sure to break in, and to appropriate the empty canvass. Pain will dictate our anticipation, and a posthumous life will be apprehended as replete with the most terrible concomitants which such a counsellor can suggest.

Besides, pain alone, and want or uneasiness, which is a species of pain, are the standing provisions of nature. Even the mode of appeasing those wants, is the discovery of human skill; what is called *pleasure* is a secondary formation, something superadded to the satisfaction of our wants by a farther reach of artifice; and only enjoyable when that satisfaction is perfect for the present, as well as prompt and certain for the future. Want and pain, therefore, are natural; satisfaction and pleasure, artificial and invented: and the former will on this ground also be more likely to present itself as the characteristic of an unknown state, than the latter.

The preceding arguments seem to evince most satisfactorily, that a posthumous existence, if really anticipated, is far more likely to be conceived as a state of suffering, than of enjoyment. Such anticipation, therefore, considered in itself, and without any reference to the direction which it gives to human conduct, will assuredly occasion more misery than happiness to those who entertain it.

Though believers in a posthumous existence seldom in fact anticipate its joys or torments as unconditionally awaiting them, and altogether independent of their present conduct, yet it is important to examine the effects and tendency of the belief, when thus entertained. We frequently hear the hope of immortality magnified as one of the loftiest privileges and blessings of human nature, without which man would be left in a state of mournful and comfortless destitution. To all these vague declamations, by which it is attempted to interest the partiality of mankind in favour of the belief in question, the foregoing arguments furnish a reply; they demonstrate that such anticipations, so far from conferring happiness on mankind, are certain to fasten in preference upon prospects of torments, and to occasion a large overplus of apprehension and uneasiness—at least until some revelation intervenes to settle and define them, and to terminate that ignorance which casts so terrific a character over the expected scenes.

He who imagines himself completely mortal, suffers no apprehension or misery, in this life, from the prospect of death, except that which the pains attending it, and the loss of present enjoyments, unavoidably hold out. A posthumous existence, if anticipated as blissful, would doubtless greatly alleviate the disquietude which the prospect of death occasions. It cannot be denied that such a persuasion would prove the source of genuine happiness to the believer. But the fact is, that a posthumous existence is not, by the majority of believers, anticipated as thus blissful, but as replete with terrors. The principles of human nature, to which reference has been made in the foregoing arguments, completely warrant this conclusion, supposing no revelation at hand to instil and guarantee more consoling hopes. It is obvious therefore, that natural religion, alone and unassisted, will to the majority of its believers materially aggravate the disquietude occasioned by the prospect of death. Instead of soothing apprehensions which cannot be wholly dispelled, it would superadd fresh grounds of uneasiness, wrapped up in an uncertainty which only renders them more painful and depressing.

Having thus ascertained, that posthumous anticipations, considered in themselves and in their capacity of feelings, occasion more unhappiness than benefit to the believer, I shall now examine them under that point of view in which they are commonly regarded as most beneficial and valuable.

CHAPTER III

The Expectations of posthumous Pain and Pleasure, which Natural Religion holds out, considered as conditional, and as exercising influence upon human Conduct.

It is in this mode that such expectations are commonly regarded as most beneficial to mankind. The anticipation of posthumous pleasure and pain, conditional upon the actions of the believer, is affirmed to imprint upon individual conduct a bias favourable to the public happiness. I shall now proceed to investigate the validity of this plea, which has hitherto been seldom challenged.

If natural religion contributes to human happiness, by means of the influence which it exercises on the conduct of men, such a result can be brought about only in one of these ways; Either it must provide *a directive rule*, communicating the knowledge of the *right path*—or it must furnish *a sanction* or inducement for the observance of some directive rule, supposed to be known from other sources. Unless it thus either admonishes or impels, it cannot possibly affect in any way the course of human nature.

SECTION I—NATURAL RELIGION FURNISHES NO DIRECTIVE RULE WHATEVER.

It is obvious at first sight, that natural religion communicates to mankind no rule of guidance. This is the leading defect which revelation is stated to supply, by providing an authentic enumeration of those acts to which future pains and pleasures are annexed. Independent of revelation, it cannot be pretended that there exists any standard, to which the believer in a posthumous existence, can apply for relief and admonition. The whole prospect is wrapt in impenetrable gloom, nor is there a streak of light to distinguish the one true path of future happiness from the infinite possibilities of error with which it is surrounded.

Nor is the absence of any authoritative collection of rules, by which the believer might adjust his steps in all circumstances however difficult, the only defect to be remarked. Experience imparts no information upon the subject. That watchful scout, who on all other occasions spies out the snares and terrors of the march, and points out the path of comparative safety, here altogether deserts us. We search in vain for any witness who may enlighten this deplorable ignorance. The distribution of these pains and pleasures is completely unseen, nor does either the gainer or loser ever return to testify the mode of dispensing them. We cannot therefore pretend even to conjecture whether there is any general rule observed in awarding them; or if there be a rule, what are its dictates. It is impossible to divine what behaviour is visited with severity, what conduct leads to pleasurable results, during a state in which there is not a glimmering of light to guide us.

The natural religionist therefore is not only destitute of any previous official warning, by a compliance with which he may ensure safety or favour: He has not even the means of consulting those decisions according to which the pleasures and pains are actually awarded to actions already committed. Not only is there no statute law extant, distinguishing, with that strict precision which should characterise the legislator as he ought to be, the path of happiness from that of misery: even the imperfect light of common law is here extinguished—even that record of decisions is forbidden, from whence we might at least borrow some shadowy and occasional surmises, and learn to steer clear of the more excruciating lots of pain. The darkness is desperate and unfathomable; and as truth and rectitude can be but a single track amidst an infinity of divergent errors, the chances in favour of a wrong line of conduct are perfectly incalculable. Yet a false step, if once committed, is altogether without hope or remedy. For when the posthumous sufferings are inflicted, the hour of application and profit is irrevocably past, and the sufferer enjoys not even the melancholy consolation which he might derive from the hope of preventing any future repetition of the same torture.

It seems, therefore, almost unaccountable, that natural religion how rich soever its promises, how terrible soever its threats, should exercise the least influence upon human conduct, since the conditions of its awards are altogether veiled from our sight. Why does the prospect of other pains affect our conduct? Because experience teaches us the actions to which they are specially attached. Until we acquire this knowledge, our behaviour cannot possibly be actuated by the anticipations which they create. How then can natural religion, shrouded as it is in such matchless obscurity, prove an exception to these infallible principles, and impel mankind without specifying a single benefit derivable from one course of action rather than another?

Since however it unquestionably does exercise some influence upon human conduct, this must be effected by providing inducements for some extraneous directive rule. I shall proceed to examine the nature of the precepts which it thus adopts and enforces, since there are none peculiarly suggested by itself.

SECTION II—NATURAL RELIGION INDIRECTLY SUGGESTS, AND APPLIES HER INDUCEMENTS TO THE OBSERVANCE OF, A RULE OF ACTION VERY PERNICIOUS TO THE TEMPORAL INTERESTS OF MANKIND.

In inquiring what extraneous rules of conduct are likely to promise either posthumous pleasure, or security from posthumous pain, we are unable to perceive, at first, how the believer should be led to any preference or conclusion upon the subject. So completely are we destitute of evidence, that it seems presumptuous to select any one mode of conduct, or, to exclude any other. Experience alone can announce to us what behaviour is attended with enjoyment or discomfort during this life; It is this guide alone who informs us that the taste of fruit will procure pleasure, or that contact with the fire will occasion pain, and if the trial had never been made, we should to this day have remained ignorant even of these trite and familiar facts. We could not have affirmed or denied any thing about them. Suppose a species of fruit perfectly new to be discovered; If any one, before, either he himself, or some one else has tasted it, confidently pronounces that it is sweet and well flavoured, an assertion so premature and uncertified could be treated only with contempt. We should term it folly and presumption thus to prophecy the pleasure or pain consequent *in this life* upon any particular conduct, prior to any experimental test. Whence comes it then, that the same certificate which is allowed to be our only safeguard here against the dreams and chimeras of fancy, should be dismissed as superfluous and unnecessary in our anticipations of posthumous pain and pleasure? If a man ignorant of medicine is unable to point out a course of life which shall, if pursued in England, preserve him from liability to the yellow fever when he goes to Jamaica, how much more boldness is required to prescribe a preparatory course against consequences still farther removed from the possibility of conjecture?

Rash, however, as such anticipations may seem to be, they have almost universally obtained reception, under some form or other. And it is highly important to trace the leading assumptions which have governed the prophesies of men on the subject of posthumous pain and pleasure—to detect those universal principles which never fail to stand out amidst an infinite variety of subordinate accompaniments.

Natural religion merely implants in a man the expectation of a posthumous existence, involving awards of enjoyment and suffering apportioned by an invisible Being. This we suppose it to assure and certify; beyond this, all is dark and undiscovered. But on a subject so dim and yet so terrible, the obtrusive conjectures of fancy will not be silenced, and she will proceed to particularise and interpolate without delay. The character of the invisible Being in whose hands these fearful dispensations are lodged, will present the most plausible theme for her speculations. If his temper, and the actions with which he is pleased or displeased, can be once discovered, an apparent clue to the secret sentences of futurity will be obtained. He will gratify those whose conduct he likes; injure those whose behaviour is disagreeable to him. But what modes of conduct will he be supposed to approve or disapprove?

Before we proceed to unfold the principles which govern our suppositions regarding the temper, it may be important to point out, in a few words, the insufficient basis upon which all anticipations of future enjoyment or suffering are built, independent of revelation. The pains and pleasures of a posthumous life are under the dispensation of the invisible Being. But so also are the pains and pleasures of this life. You do not found any expectations regarding the latter upon any assumed disposition of their invisible Dispenser. You do not pacify your ignorance of those causes which may create a tendency to the yellow fever, by conjecturing that certain actions are displeasing to his feelings. Predictions founded upon such wretched surmise would indicate the meanest imbecility. Why then should such evidence be considered as sanctioning anticipations of posthumous awards, when the commonest experience will not allow it to be employed to interpret the dispensations of the very same Being in the present life? In estimating the chances of life and death, of health and disease, no insurer ever inquires whether the actions of the applicant have been agreeable or disagreeable to the Deity. And the reasoning, upon which the trial by ordeal rests, is regarded with unqualified contempt, implying as it does, that this Being approves or detests modes of action, and that he will manifest these feelings by dispensations in this life, of favour or severity. Yet this is merely a consistent application of the very same shift, for superseding the necessity of experience, on which the posthumous prophecies of natural religion are founded.

In this life, however, it may be urged, there are laws of nature which the Deity cannot or will not interrupt. But why should there not also be posthumous laws of nature, discoverable only by experience of them, and inviolable to the same extent? The presumption unquestionably is, that there are such posthumous laws, and that we can no more predict, from a reference to the attributes of the Deity, the modes of acquiring pleasure and avoiding pain in a posthumous life, than we can in this.

Amidst the dimness and distance of futurity, however, reason is altogether struck blind, and we do not scruple to indulge in these baseless anticipations. The assumed character of the invisible Dispenser is the only ground on which fancy can construct her scale of posthumous promotion and disgrace. And thus the rule of action, to which natural religion will affix her inducements of future vengeance and remuneration, will be framed entirely upon the conceptions entertained regarding his character.

We thus find ourselves somewhat nearer to the object of the present enquiry, whether natural religion conduces to the happiness or misery of mankind during the present life; It appears that natural religion does not itself originate any rule of action whatever, and that the rule which it is supposed to second and enforce depends only upon conceptions of the temper of the Deity. If he is conceived to be perfectly beneficent—having no personal affections of his own, or none but such as are coincident with the happiness of mankind—patronising those actions alone which are useful, and exactly in the degree in which they are useful—detesting in a similar manner and proportion those which are hurtful—then the actions agreeable to him will be beneficial to mankind, and inducements to the performance of them will promote the happiness of mankind. If, on the other hand, he is depicted as unbeneficent—as having personal affections seldom coincident with human happiness, frequently injurious to it, and almost always frivolous and exactive—favouring actions which are not useful at all, or not in the degree in which they are useful—disapproving with the same caprice and without any reference to utility—then the course of action by which his favour is to be sought, will be more or less injurious to mankind, and inducements to pursue it will in the present life tend to the production of unhappiness.

From this alternative there can be no escape. According to the temper of the Being whom we seek to please, will be the mode of conduct proper for conciliating his favour. To serve the devil is universally considered as implying the most abhorrent and detestable behaviour.

If we consult the language in which mankind speak of the Deity, we shall be led to imagine that he is in their conception a being of perfect and unsullied beneficence, uniting in himself all that is glorious and all that is amiable. Such is the tendency and amount of the words which they employ. Strange, however, as the inconsistency may appear, it will not be difficult to demonstrate, that mere natural religion invariably leads its votaries to ascribe to their Deity a character of caprice and tyranny, while they apply to him, at the same moment, all those epithets of eulogy and reverence which their language comprises. This discrepancy between the actual and the pretended conception is an infallible result of the circumstances, and agreeable to the principles of human nature.

1. What are the fundamental data, as communicated by natural religion, respecting the Deity, from which his temper and inclinations are to be inferred? A power to which we can assign no limits—an agency which we are unable to comprehend or frustrate—such are the original attributes from which the disposition of the possessor is to be gathered.

Now the feeling which excessive power occasions in those who dwell under its sway, is extreme and unmixed fear. This is its appropriate and never failing effect, and he who could preserve an undisturbed aspect in the face of a power against which he knew of no protection, and which might destroy him in an instant, would justly be extolled as a man of heroic firmness. But what is the temper of mind which fear presupposes in the object which excites it? A disposition to do harm. Now a disposition to do harm, conjoined to the power of effecting it at pleasure, constitutes the very essence of tyranny. Examine the fictitious narratives respecting men of extraordinary strength; You will find a Giant or a Cyclops uniformly pourtrayed as cruel in the extreme, and delighted with the scent of human blood. Such are the dispositions which the human fancy naturally imagines as guiding the employment of irresistible might. Our terrors (as Father Malebranche remarks) justify themselves, by suggesting appropriate persuasions of impending evil, and compel us to regard the possessor of unlimited powers as a tyrant.

The second characteristic of the Deity is an unknown and incomprehensible agency. Now an incomprehensible mode of behaviour, not reducible to any known principles, is in human affairs termed *caprice*, when confined to the trifling occurrences of life; *insanity*, when it extends to important occasions. The capricious or the insane are those whose proceedings we cannot reconcile with the acknowledged laws of human conduct—those whose conduct defies our utmost sagacity of prediction. They are incomprehensible agents endued with limited power. The epithets *capricious, insane, incomprehensible*, are perfectly convertible and synonymous.

Let experience now teach us the feelings with which mankind usually regard the mad, the wayward, and the unfathomable course of proceeding among themselves. They laugh at the caprices of a child; they tremble at the incoherent speech and gestures of a madman. Every one shrinks with dismay from the presence of the latter; the laws instantly enclose his body, and thrust upon it the invincible manacles of matter, since no known apprehension will act as a sufficient coercive upon his mind. Caprice and insanity, when accompanied even with the limited strength of a man, excite in us the keenest alarm, which is only heightened by the indefinite shape of the coming evil.

But let us suppose this object of our terror to be still farther strengthened. What if we arm the incomprehensible man with a naked sword! What if we figure him, like the insane Orlando of Ariosto, roaming about with an invulnerable hide, and limbs insensible to the chain! What if, still farther, he be entrusted with the government of millions, seconded by irresistible legions who stand ready at his beck! Can the utmost stretch of fancy produce any picture so appalling, as that of a mad, capricious, and incomprehensible Being exalted to this overwhelming sway? Yet this terrific representation involves nothing beyond surpassing might, wielded by one whose agency is unfathomable. And these are the two attributes, the alliance of which, in a measure still more fearful and unlimited, constitutes the Deity, as pourtrayed by natural religion.

So complete is this identity between incomprehensible conduct and madness, that amongst early nations, the madman is supposed to be under the immediate inspiration and controul of the Deity, whose agency is always believed to commence where coherent and rational behaviour terminates.

But the Deity (it will be urged) treats us with favour and kindness, and this may suffice to remove our apprehensions of him. I reply, that the most valuable gift could never efface them, while the proceedings of the donor continued to be entirely inconsistent and unintelligible. It is the very essence of caprice and madness, that present behaviour constitutes no security whatever for the future. Our disquietude for the future must therefore remain as oppressive as before, and can never be relieved by these occasional gusts of transient good-humour. As few men hope, and almost every one fears, in cases where no assured calculation can be framed, it is obvious that this irregular favouritism would still leave us in all the restlessness of suspense and uncertainty.

The actual conception, therefore, which mankind will form of the Deity, from the consideration of those original data which unassisted natural religion promulgates concerning him, seems now to be sufficiently determined. He will not be conceived as designing constant and unmixed evil, for otherwise his power would carry it into effect; nor, for the same reason, as meditating universal and unceasing good. While there exists good in the universe, such a power cannot be wielded by perfect malevolence; while there exists evil, it cannot be directed by consummate benevolence.[1] Besides, either of these two suppositions would destroy

1. Plato tells us that the Deity is perfectly and systematically well intentioned, but that he was prevented from realizing these designs, by the inherent badness and intractable qualities of matter. This supposition does indeed vindicate the intentions of the supreme Being, but only by grievously insulting his power and limiting his omnipotence. According to this theory, the Deity becomes a perfectly *comprehensible* person; and the attribute of incom-

the attribute of incomprehensibility, and would substitute in their stead a consecutive and intelligible system of action. The Deity therefore will be conceived as fluctuating between the two; sometimes producing evil, sometimes good, but infinitely more as an object of terror than of hope. His changeful and incomprehensible inclinations will be supposed more frequently pernicious than beneficial to mankind, and the portrait of a capricious tyrant will thus be completed.

2. Unamiable, however, and appalling as this conception may actually be, it is equally undeniable that no language, except that of the most devoted reverence and eulogy, will ever be employed in describing or addressing the Deity. To demonstrate this, it will be necessary to revert to the origin of praise and blame.

Praise is the expression of goodwill and satisfaction towards the person who has occassioned us a certain pleasure. It intimates a readiness on our part to manifest this goodwill by some farther repayment. It supposes the performance of a service which we have neither the right to expect, nor the means of exacting. We bestow it in order to evince to the performer of the service and to the public in general, that we are not insensible to the favour

---

prehensibility being taken away, all the preceding reasonings which are founded on it fall to the ground. But at the same time that he becomes perfectly comprehensible, he becomes a thorough dead letter with regard to all human desires and expectations. For by the supposition his power only extends to the production of the already existing amount of good. He can produce no more good—that is, he can be of no farther use to any one, and therefore it is vain to trouble ourselves about him.

But what evidence is there for this doctrine of Plato? Not the shadow of an argument can be produced in its favour, and where nothing is set up as a defence, one cannot tell where to aim an attack. The only mode of assailing it is by constructing a similar phantom on one's own side, in order to expose the absurdity of the first by its resemblance to the second. Conformably to this rule, I affirm that the Deity is perfectly and systematically malevolent, and that he was only prevented from realising these designs by the inherent goodness and incorruptible excellence of matter. I admit that there is not the smallest evidence for this, but it is just as well supported, and just as probable as the preceding theory of Plato.

received, and that we are disposed to view all who thus benefit us with peculiar complacency. Our praise therefore is destined to operate as a stimulus to the repetition of that behaviour by which we profit.

Blame, on the contrary, is the signal of dissatisfaction and wrath against the person who has caused us pain. It implies a disposition which would be gratified by inflicting injury upon him. It proclaims to him, and to every one else, our sense of the hurt, and the perils prepared for all who treat us in a similar manner. And we design, by means of it, to frighten and deter every one from conduct noxious to our welfare.

Such is the origin and such the intention of the language of encomium and dispraise. Each is a species of sanction, vested in the hands of every individual, and employed by him for his own benefit; the former *remuneratory*, and destined to encourage the manifestation of kindness towards him; the latter *punitory*, and intended to prevent injurious treatment.

Having thus unfolded the nature of praise and censure, it will not be difficult to explain the laws which govern their application; and to separate the circumstances in which a man will praise, from those in which he will blame.

Our employment of the punitory sanction, or of blame, is in exact proportion to our power; our employment of the remuneratory sanction, or of praise, is in a similar manner proportional to our weakness.

The man of extraordinary power, who possesses unlimited disposal of the instruments of terror, has not the slightest motive to praise. His blame, the herald and precursor of impending torture, is abundantly sufficient to ensure conformity to his will. The remuneratory sanction is in its nature comparatively feeble and uncertain; the punitory, when applied in sufficient magnitude, is altogether infallible and omnipotent. He who possesses an adequate command of the latter, will never condescend to make use of the former. He will regard himself as strictly entitled to the most unqualified subservience on the part of those whom he might in an instant plunge into excruciating torments. If he partially waives the exercise of this prerogative, he will consider it as an undeserved extension of mercy.

On the other hand, the man without strength or influence, who cannot hurt us even if he wished it, is cut off from the employment of the punitory sanction. His blame is an impotent murmur, threatening no future calamity, and therefore listened to with indifference. It would, under these circumstances, revolt and irritate us, or else provoke our derision. In either case, it would only render us less disposed to conform to his will, and policy therefore will induce him to repress it altogether. His sole method of influencing our behaviour is by a prodigal employment of the remuneratory sanction—by repaying the slightest favour with unbounded expressions of gratitude—by lavishing upon us such loud and devoted eulogy, as may impress us with his readiness to consecrate to our benefit all the energies of a human being, if we condescend to repeat our kindness. Such are the methods by which he endeavours to magnify and exaggerate the slender bounty which fortune permits him to apply in encouragement of the favours of mankind.

The most copious experience may be adduced in support of these principles. Does the planter, whom the law arms with unlimited power, bestow any eulogy upon his slave, in return for the complete monopoly of his whole life and services? He considers himself as entitled to *demand* all this, since he possesses the means of *extorting* its fulfilment. Let us trace the descending scale of power, and mark how the approach of weakness gradually unsheaths the remuneratory sanction. Were his free labourer (particularly in those lands where labour is scarce and highly paid) to work in his employment with an energy and devotion at all comparable to that which he exacts from his slave, the planter would be prompt in applying the stimulus and encouragement of eulogy. A slighter service, on the part of a friend of equal rank, will draw from him encomiums on the kind and generous temper by which he has benefited. But the merest civility, even a peculiar look or word, bestowed by the king or a superior, is sufficient to impress upon him the deepest esteem and reverence. He loudly extols the gracious department of a person upon whom he had no claim, and from whom he could have entertained no expectations.

If any one makes me a present of a considerable sum, I magnify his bounty to the skies; I recommend him to the public by all the epithets significant of kindly and beneficent feelings, and thus display the conspicuous return which I am ready to make for such treatment. But let the government grant me a claim upon his estate, however unjustly, and the premium of praise is no longer necessary when I am thus master of the engine of exaction. I no longer therefore bestow upon him, by whose labour I profit, those laudatory terms which promise good will on my part. "Is it not enough for him" (said Charles I when the death of Lord Northampton was commended to his sympathy)—"Is it not enough that he has died for his king?" So thoroughly is the standing demand which any one makes upon his fellow-creatures, measured by the extent of his compulsory power. It is upon those services only, which overstep this limit, and which he possesses not the means of extorting, that he will expend the tribute of his praise, or waste the incentive which it offers to a future reproduction of favours. Charles I would not have uttered such a sentence the day before his execution.

With the weak, again, the punitory sanction is completely silenced and annulled. A slave never dreams of announcing dissatisfaction at the conduct of his master. If he did so, the consequence would be an additional infliction of stripes. In despotic governments you hear not a murmur against the oppressor—at least, until excess of suffering produces desperation. The entire extinction of all free sentiment among dependants and courtiers has become proverbial. They dare not express even that indirect and qualified censure of their superior, which is implied in dissenting from his opinion. They tolerate his insults with a patience and complacency for which they reimburse themselves in their conversation with inferiors. Not only do they abstain from hinting that there is any censurable ingredient in his character, but they dare not even withhold their encomiums, lest they should seem to doubt his exalted merit. It is unnecessary to cite particular instances of a subservience and flattery so notorious.

In proportion as we raise the inferior into equality, his blame becomes more efficacious, and is proclaimed oftener and more freely. Advance him still higher, and his propensity to find fault will be still farther extended, until at last it becomes so exciteable and eruptive, as to disregard altogether the feelings of others, and to visit with merciless severity the most trivial defect of conformity to his wishes.

From this examination we may extract some important principles, which will materially elucidate the object of the present enquiry. It appears, first, that the employment of praise or blame bears an exact ratio to the comparative weakness or strength of the critic. Weakness determines praise, strength blame; and the force of either sentiment is measured by the extent of the determining quality. The greater the disparity of power, the more severe is the blame heaped upon the inferior, and more excessive the praise lavished upon the superior. Secondly, the employment of praise and blame is in an inverse ratio to each other. He who praises the most, blames the least; he who blames the most, scarcely praises at all. The man to whom the utmost praise is addressed, seldom hears any blame—and *vice versâ*. Thirdly, the application of praise and blame bears an inverse ratio to the services performed. The greater the service rendered, the more is the performer of it blamed; the less is he praised. There is no human being from whom the planter derives so much benefit as from his slave; there is none upon whom he expends so little eulogy, or pours so much reproach. On the contrary, it is towards him who has the largest power of inflicting evil upon us, and who confers on us the most insignificant favours, that our encomiums are the warmest, our censure the most gentle and sparing. A mere intermission of the whip, or perhaps an occasional holiday, will draw forth abundant expression of praise on the part of the slave. How gracious and beneficent is a sovereign styled, by him upon whom he has bestowed a single look of favour! The vehemence of our praise is thus not measured by the extent of the kindness bestowed, but by the superiority of the donor to the receiver, and implies only the dependence and disparity of the latter.

If the foregoing account of praise and blame be correct, it presents an entire solution of the apparent discrepancy which suggested itself at the commencement of the enquiry. It explains how the Deity, although actually conceived (from the mere data of natural religion) as a capricious despot, is yet never described or addressed without the largest and most prodigal encomiums. For where is the case in which so tremendous an exaltation of the agent above the subject can be pointed out? Where is the comparative weakness of the latter so deplorably manifest? The power of which we speak is unlimited, and therefore with respect to it, we are altogether prostrate and abject. It is, under such circumstances, the natural course, that we should abstain from all disparaging and provocative epithets, and repress every whisper which might indicate a tone of disaffection towards the Omnipotent. "Personne n'aime a prendre une peine inutile, même un enfant," observes Rousseau; and to proclaim an impotent hatred, besides being unmeaning and irrational, might prove positively noxious, by alienating any inclination to benefit us on the part of the Supreme. However painful may be the treatment which we experience at his hands, we must cautiously refrain from pronouncing our genuine sentiments of the injury, inasmuch as such a freedom might prolong or aggravate, but could never extenuate, our sufferings.

The same weakness will give birth to an extravagant and unsparing use of the remuneratory sanction. We know well how little our epithets really signify or promise, since the Deity stands in no need of our good offices; and therefore we endeavour to bestow force upon this host of unmeaning effusions by multiplying its numbers, and by piling up superlative upon superlative. We magnify the smallest crumb into a splendid benefaction, which merits on our part a return of endless devotion to his service. By thus testifying our own ready subservience—by applying to him terms significant of qualities morally good and beneficial to mankind, and thereby intimating that every one else owes to him a similar gratitude—we hope to constitute something like a motive for repeating the favour. This varied and exuberant flattery is the only mode of soothing the irritability of an earthly despot; and therefore we naturally apply it to one of still more surpassing might.

Suppose that any tyrant could establish so complete a system of espionage, as to be informed of every word which any of his subjects might utter: It is obvious that all criticisms upon him would be laudatory in the extreme, for they would be all pronounced as it were in the presence of the tyrant, and *there* we know that no one dares to express even dissent of opinion. The unlimited agency of the Deity is equivalent to this universal espionage. He is conceived as the unseen witness of every thing which passes our lips—indeed even of our thoughts. It would be madness, therefore, to hazard an unfavourable judgment of his proceedings, while thus constantly under his supervision.

It seems, therefore, sufficiently demonstrated, that the same incomprehensible power, which would cause the Deity to be conceived as a capricious despot, would also occasion him to be spoken of only under titles of the loftiest eulogy. For language is not the sign of the idea actually existing in the mind of the speaker—but of that which he desires to convey to the hearer. In the present case these two ideas are completely at variance, as they must uniformly be where there is an excessive disparity of power.

It has been necessary to pursue the enquiry into the character of the Deity, as pourtrayed by natural religion, to a length which may possibly seem tedious. But as the rule of conduct, to which natural religion applies her inducements, depends altogether on the conceptions framed of the invisible governor of a posthumous existence—it is of the highest moment to lay bare the actual conceptions of him, in order to ascertain whether a behaviour adjusted according to them will be beneficial or injurious to mankind.

Since the dispositions of the Deity are, in this unenlightened condition, supposed to be thus capricious and incomprehensible, it may seem extraordinary that mankind should have attempted to assign to them a definite boundary, by marking out any line of conduct as agreeable or disagreeable to him.

But the fact is, that the terms incomprehensible and unlimited are merely negative, and therefore have no positive meaning whatever: Their actual import is, that the Deity is a being of whom we know less, and who has more power, than any other. We conceive him as differing only in degree from other possessors of power, and we therefore assimilate him the most closely to those earthly sovereigns in whom the most irresistible might resides.

We are thus furnished with a clue to the actions which unassisted natural religion will represent as agreeable and odious to the Deity. Experience announces to us what practices will recommend us to the favour of terrestrial potentates, and what will provoke their enmity. From this analogy (the nearest we can attain upon the subject) will be copied the various modes of behaviour which the Deity is imagined to favour or abominate. To pursue the former course and avoid the latter, will be the directive rule to which the inducements of natural religion affix themselves. This directive rule will indeed ramify into many accidental shapes, among different nations; but its general tenor and spirit will, throughout, be governed by the analogy just mentioned, since that is our nearest resource and substitute in the total silence of experience.

The central passion in the mind of a despot is an insatiate love of dominion, and thirst for its increase. All his approbation and disapprobation, all his acts of reward and punishment, are wholly dictated by this master-principle. I state this in a broad and unqualified manner; but I feel warranted by the amplest evidence, and by the concurrent testimony of political writers, almost all of whom stigmatise in the harshest language the unbridled government of a single man.

Pursuing this clue, it will not be difficult to distinguish those characters which he will mark out as estimable or hateful. The foremost in his estimation will be that man who most essentially contributes to the maintenance of his power: the greatest object of his hatred will be he who most eminently threatens its annihilation. Next in the catalogue of merit will be inserted the person who can impress upon his mind, in the most vivid and forcible manner, the delicious conviction of his supremacy—who can re-kindle this association continually, and strike out new modes of application to prevent it from subsiding into indifference. Next in the list of demerit will appear the name of him, whose conduct tends to invalidate this consciousness of overwhelming might—whose open defiance or tardy conformity generates mistrust and apprehension—or who, at least, can contemplate with an unterrified and uninfluenced eye the whole apparatus of majesty. Such will be the most eminent subjects, both of favour and disgrace, on the part of the despot.

In all cases where the gratification of his love of power is allied with the happiness of his subjects, qualities conducive to that happiness will recommend themselves to his patronage. But it is a melancholy truth, that this coincidence *seldom*, we might say *never*, occurs. He who is thus absorbed in love of dominion, cannot avoid loving the correlative and inseparable event—the debasement of those over whom he rules; in order that his own supremacy may become more pointed and prominent. Of course he also has an interest in multiplying their privations, which are the symptoms and measure of that debasement. Besides, his leading aim is to diffuse among his subjects the keenest impressions of his own power. This is, in other words, to plant in their bosoms an incessant feeling of helplessness, insecurity and fear; and were this aim realized, every thing which deserves the name of happiness must, throughout their lives, be altogether over shadowed and stifled.

Doubtless there will be occasions on which the view of prosperity will gratify him. Such will be the case when it is strongly associated with the exercise of his own creative fiat—and when its dependance upon and derivation from himself is so glaring as to blazon forth conspicuously the majesty of the donor. In order thus to affect the public mind, his benefits must be rare in their occurrence, bestowed only on a few, and concentrated into striking and ostentatious masses. All the prosperity, therefore, in which he will take an interest will be that of a few favourites; his own work, achieved by the easy process of donation. This munificence of temper, however, is not only not coincident with the happiness of the community, but is altogether hostile to it. The former, because the real welfare of the many is to be secured not by occasional fits of kindness, but by the slow and unobtrusive effect of systematic regulations, built upon this study of human nature, discoverable only by patient thought, and requiring perpetual watchfulness in their application: The latter, because these donatives are at the bottom mere acts of spoliation, snatching away the labours of the many for the benefit of a favoured few.

It thus plainly appears that the despot can never derive any pleasure from the genuine well being of the community, though he may at times gratify himself by exalting individuals to sudden pre-eminence over the rest. Consequently the qualities conducive to the happiness of the community will not meet with the smallest encouragement from him. They will even be discouraged, indirectly at least, by the preference shewn to other qualities not contributory to this end. But the personal affections of the despot have been shewn to lead, in almost all cases, to the injury of the people. And therefore those mental habits, which tend to gratify these affections, will be honoured with his unqualified approval; those which tend to frustrate them, will incur his detestation. In the former catalogue will be comprised all the qualities which lessen and depress human happiness; in the latter, all which foster and improve it.

Such is the scale according to which the praise and censure, the rewards and punishments, of the earthly potentate, will be dispensed. By this model, the nearest which experience presents, the conceptions of mankind must be guided, in conjecturing the character and inclinations of the Deity.

The first place in the esteem of the Deity will, in pursuance of this analogy, be allotted to those who disseminate his influence among men—who are most effectually employed in rendering his name dreaded and reverenced, and enforcing the necessity of perpetual subjection to him. Priests, therefore, whose lives are devoted to this object, will be regarded as the most favoured class.

The largest measure of his hate will in like manner be supposed to devolve on those, who attempt to efface these apprehensions, and to render mankind independent of him, by removing the motives for this subjection. The most decisive way of effecting this is by presuming to call in question his existence—an affront of peculiar poignancy, to which the material despot is not exposed. Atheists, therefore, will be the person whom he is imagined to view with the most signal abomination.

Immediately beneath the priests will be placed those who manifest the deepest and most permanent sense of his agency and power—in words, by the unceasing use of hyperbole, to extol the Deity and depress themselves—in action, by abstaining on his account from agreeable occupations, and performing ceremonies which can be ascribed to no other motive than the desire of pleasing him. Works, which can be ascribed to this motive alone, must from their very nature produce no good at all, or at least very little: for were they thus beneficial, they would be recompensed with the esteem and gratitude of mankind, and the performer of them might be suspected of having originally aimed at this independent advantage. Whereas he who whips himself every night, or prefaces every mouthful with a devotional formula, can hardly be supposed to have contemplated the smallest temporal profit, or to have had any other end in view, than that of pleasing the Deity. Such actions will be thought to convey to him the liveliest testimony of his own unparalleled influence, and the performers of them will be placed second in the scale of merit.

Next to Atheists, his highest displeasure will be conceived to attach to those who either avowedly brave his power, or tacitly slight and disregard it—who indulge in language of irreverent censure, or withhold the daily offering of their homage and prostration—who dwell careless of his supremacy, and decline altogether the endurance of privations from which no known benefit, either to themselves or others, can arise. Such persons assume an independence which silently implies that the arm of the Deity is shortened and cannot reach them; and they will, therefore, be considered as the next objects of his indignation.

These then are the qualities, which the natural religionist, guided by the experience of temporal potentates, will imagine the Deity to favour or dislike. To this extraneous directive rule, therefore, the inducements of natural religion, and the expectations of a posthumous life, will apply themselves. Nor can we doubt, for an instant, that such a rule is highly detrimental to human happiness in this life.

It cannot be otherwise, so long as nothing more is known of the Deity except that he possesses a superhuman power, and that we cannot understand his course of action. It is the essence of power to exact obedience; and obedience involves privation and suffering on the part of the inferior. The Deity having power over all mankind, exacts an obedience co-extensive with his power; therefore all mankind must obey him, or, in other words, immolate to his supremacy a certain portion of their happiness. He loves human obedience; that is, he is delighted with human privations and pain, for these are the test and measure of obedience. He is pleased, when his power is felt and acknowledged: That is, he delights to behold a sense of abasement, helplessness, and terror, prevalent among mankind. If, under the earthly despot, rewards and punishments are undeniably distributed in a manner injurious to human happiness—under the God of unassisted natural religion, whose attributes must be borrowed from the despot, the case must be similar. There is indeed this difference which deserves to be remarked—that those deductions from human happiness which the temporal potentate requires, are altogether unproductive and final: While those exacted by the Deity, though embracing the very same period, are in comparison transient and preparatory, entitling the contracting party to the amplest posthumous reimbursement. In the former case, the expenditure of suffering is a dead loss; in the latter, it is a judicious surrender of present, in expectation of future, advantages.

But it may be urged in opposition, that the Deity is like a beneficent judge, and not like a despot—that he fetters individual taste no farther than is necessary for the happiness of the whole. Revelation may doubtless thus characterise him; but natural religion can never pourtray him under this amiable aspect. His power is irresistible, and therefore all limitations of it must be voluntary and self-imposed. How then can we venture to assume, that he will exact from individuals no more self-denial that is requisite for the benefit of the whole, unless it shall please him specially to communicate to us his recognition of such a boundary? We cannot possibly know what boundary he will select, until he informs us. Prior to revelation, therefore, the Deity can be conceived as nothing else but a despot—that is, the possessor of unrestricted sway. To compare him with a beneficent judge, is an analogy wholly fallacious and inadmissible. Why is the judge beneficent? Because his power is derivative, dependent and responsible. Why does he impose upon individuals no farther sacrifices than are necessary to ensure the well being of the society? Because all the compulsory force which he can employ is borrowed from the society, who will not permit it to be used for other purposes. Suppose these circumstances altered, and that the judge possesses himself of independent unresponsible power: The result is, that he becomes a despot, and ceases altogether to be beneficent. It is only when thus strengthened and unshackled that he becomes a proper object of comparison with the Deity—and then, instead of a judge, he degenerates invariably into an oppressor and a tyrant.

Amongst other expressions of reverence towards the Deity, doubtless the appellation of a judge, one of the most adorable functions which can grace humanity, will not be omitted. But we have already shewn that the language of praise is not on this occasion to be considered as indicating the existence of truly valuable qualities in the object. Because that immensity of power, which is the distinguishing attribute of the Deity, distorts the epithets of eulogy, and terrifies us into an offer of them, by way of propitiation, whether deserved or not by any preceding service.

It seems clear then from the foregoing inquiry, that the posthumous hopes and fears held out by natural religion, must produce the effect of encouraging actions useless and pernicious to mankind, but agreeable to the invisible Dispenser, so far as his attributes are discoverable by unaided natural religion—and our conceptions of his character, are the only evidence on which we can even build a conjecture as to the conduct which may entail upon us posthumous happiness or misery. Whatever offers an encouragement to useless or pernicious conduct, operates indirectly to discourage that which is beneficial and virtuous. In addition, therefore, to the positive evil which these inducements force into existence of themselves, they are detrimental in another way, by stifling the growth of genuine excellence, and diverting the recompence which should be exclusively reserved for it.

CHAPTER IV

Further Considerations on the temporal usefulness of that rule of action, which the inducements of Natural Religion enforce.

Though the preceding argument, drawn from the character which unassisted reason cannot fail to ascribe to the Deity, seems amply sufficient to evince that the expected distribution of his favour and enmity is not such as to stimulate useful, and to discountenance pernicious conduct, (regarding merely the present life); yet I shall subjoin a few considerations in addition, which may tend to corroborate and enforce my principles.

1. Suppose that by any peculiar perversion of reason, all belief in a God or in a future state should die away among the votaries of some Pagan system. Is it not perfectly unquestionable, that all which had been before conceived as the injunctions of natural religion, would at once be neglected and forgotten? We need not take any trouble to demonstrate this, partly because it is so obvious a consequence, partly because it is always implied in the outcry raised against atheistical writings.

But the sources of pleasure and of pain, in this community, would still remain unaltered with regard to the present life, even in the state of impiety into which they had just plunged. What had been useful or pernicious to them before, would still continue to be so. They would have precisely the same motive to encourage the former and to repress the latter. Can any reason be given why their rewards and punishments should be insufficient to effect this end? There will still, therefore, remain in the bosom of each individual, ample motive to behaviour beneficial to the society—ample motive against conduct injurious to it.

To select a particular example. He who was, before the influx of disbelief, a skilful and diligent tradesman or physician, will he on a sudden become imprudent or remiss? Will he become indifferent to the acquisition of emolument and importance? It will not surely be contended, that any such alteration of character or conduct is to be anticipated. Apply a similar supposition to the same man in other capacities—as a father, a husband, a trustee, or any other function in which the happiness of some among his fellows depends upon his conduct. In neither of these cases will there be any motive for him to deviate from his former behaviour, supposing that to have been valuable and virtuous. But all the transactions, in which a man's conduct affects his fellow-creatures, may be comprised under some relation of this sort—and in none of these situations will he have any motive to exchange a beneficial for a noxious course of action. Consequently the expiration of religious belief will leave perfectly sufficient motive for the maintenance of conduct really useful to mankind.

If the practices enjoined by natural religion would expire without its support, this must be because there is no motive left to perform them. But to say that there is no such motive, proves that the practices produce no temporal benefit whatever: E converso, therefore, he who would maintain that pious works are temporally beneficial, must also affirm, that there would be motive enough to perform them, supposing our earthly existence to terminate in annihilation. But no one ever thinks of asserting this: On the contrary, the vital necessity of implicit belief, as an incentive, is loudly proclaimed, and the certain extinction of all religious performances, if unbelief should become general, is announced and deplored. It is altogether inconsistent and contradictory, therefore, to maintain, that there is any temporal benefit annexed to these practices—since this, if true, must constitute a motive common both to believers and unbelievers.

2. If natural religion consisted in the practice of actions beneficial to mankind in the present life, the actions enjoined by it would be the same all over the earth. The sources of human pleasure and pain are similar every where, and therefore the modes of multiplying both one and the other will be similar throughout. Take, for example, any particular branch of behaviour which is justly extolled as highly conducive to human happiness: You will find justice, veracity, or prudence, precisely the same in their nature, although practised with very different degrees of strictness, both in the East, and in the West. If therefore piety consisted of a collection of qualities calculated to produce temporal benefit, you would discover the same identity between Pagan and Christian piety, as there is between Pagan and Christian justice or veracity.

But the very reverse is most notoriously the fact. The injunctions and the practices of one religion are altogether different from those of every other. Believers in any one of them will view the rest with abhorrence. A Christian who visits a country where his religion has never been heard of, will doubtless expect to meet with just or veracious men, varying in frequency according to circumstances: but he will never once dream of discovering any Christians there. Christianity therefore does not consist in the manifestation of qualities which confer temporal benefit on mankind, since these are capable of universal growth in every climate.

A mere enquiry into the meaning of words will suffice to corroborate this. When we describe an individual as belonging to any particular religion, the epithet implies that he entertains a certain set of persuasions, attested either by his own confession, or by a conformity, besides, to a peculiar class of ceremonial practices which characterize the system. But by merely indicating the religion to which he adheres, no information has been conveyed as to his moral qualities, or whether his conduct is beneficial or noxious to his fellows. It may be either one or the other, whatever be the religion he adopts or believes in. In order to state with which class it ought to be ranked, we must employ a very different language. We must describe him as a good Pagan or a bad Pagan—a just or an unjust Mussulman—veracious or a liar.

Consequently an adherence to the injunctions of religion is something entirely different from an habitual performance of beneficial actions. For the latter are every where uniform and identical, while the mandates of religion are infinitely various: And farther, in mentioning the system of religion to which any individual belongs, we do not at all state whether his conduct is beneficent or pernicious—therefore an adherence to the system is perfectly consistent either with friendship or enmity to mankind.

3. If the injunctions of piety inculcated performance or abstinence merely according as the action specified was beneficial or injurious in the present life, religion would be precisely coincident with human laws. For these latter are destined only to ensure the same end, employing temporal instead of posthumous sanctions. Religion would command and forbid the very same actions as the legislator, merely reinforcing his uncertain punishments with something more exquisite and more inevitable at the close of life. But it would give no new direction, of its own and for itself, to human conduct; It would originate no peculiar duties or crimes, but would appear simply as an auxiliary, to second and confirm that bias which the legislator would have attempted to imprint without it.

Such would have been the case had the mandates of natural religion a tendency to produce temporal happiness. How widely different is the state of the fact! Throughout the globe, under every various system, we observe the most innocuous of human pleasures criminated and interdicted by piety; pleasures such as the worst of human legislators never forbad, and never could discover any pretence for forbidding. We observe a peculiar path of merit and demerit traced out exclusively by religion—embracing numerous actions which the law has left unnoticed, and which we may therefore infer, are not recognized as deserving either reward or punishment with reference to the present life. It is altogether impossible, therefore, that the mandates of natural religion can be directed to the promotion of temporal happiness, since they diverge so strikingly from the decrees of the legislators. Whatever other end they have in view, it cannot be the same as his.

Indeed in modern times an express discussion has arisen, whether the civil magistrate can with propriety interfere at all in matters of religion. Among the more enlightened thinkers, the doctrine of toleration, or that of leaving every man to recommend himself to God by the methods which he himself prefers, so long as he abstains from injuring others, seems to be fully recognised. Scarcely any one now is found to vindicate the exaction of a forced uniformity of worship. But the very existence of the dispute decisively implies, that religion is not naturally coincident, in her injunctions, with laws—that no pious ritual is of a character tending in itself to promote the happiness of society. The intolerant party attempted to enforce the propriety of giving to law an express extension over an apparently independent province; Their opponents endeavoured to maintain this province still untouched and unregulated. If these acts could have been shewn to be productive of temporal benefit or evil, this would have been the point on which the question would have been determined, as it is with regard to other cases of human conduct. No one would have contested the necessity, in the present times at least, of interdicting any acts of worship which might consist in wounding or plundering a neighbour. But the actual point in dispute was, whether out of a number of different rituals, perfectly on a level regarding temporal profit or injury, any particular one should be singly permitted and all the rest forbidden. The argument on one side was, that the Deity preferred the species of worship which they were advocating; the other side protested against this doctrine, as an unwarranted assumption of infallibility.

It is not my purpose to enter farther into this question, and I have only adduced it in order to evince, that the mandates of religion are altogether separate in their nature and application from those of law, and therefore cannot possibly be similar in the end which they are destined to ensure—and also that this separation is virtually implied in both sides of the dispute on freedom of worship.

4. We uniformly find religious injunctions divided into two branches, the first embracing our duty to God, the second our duty to man. However beneficial may be the tendency to this latter section, it is quite impossible that the former can produce any temporal happiness. For it is, by the very definition, a rule restrictive of our conduct on those occasions when the interests of other men are not at all concerned. On these occasions the legislator would have left us unfettered, since every man naturally selects that path which is most conducive to his temporal felicity. If any other course is thrust upon him from without, it must infallibly be a sacrifice of earthly happiness.

That branch therefore, at least, of religious injunctions, which is termed *our duty to God*, must be regarded as detrimental to human felicity in this life. It is a deduction from the pleasures of the individual, without at all benefiting the species. It must be considered, so far as the present life is concerned, as a tax paid for the salutary direction which the branch termed *our duty to man* is said to imprint upon human conduct, and for the special and unequalled efficacy, with which these sanctions are alleged to operate. Supposing also the operation of this latter branch to be noxious instead of salutary, the payment of the tax will constitute so much additional evil.

CHAPTER V

Of the Efficiency of the Inducements held out by Natural Religion. How far superhuman Expectations can be regarded as likely to prove influential, where no human Inducements would be influential.

There is some difficulty in estimating exactly the extent of influence which the superhuman inducements, held out by natural religion, actually exercise over mankind. They appear always intermixed and confounded among that crowd of motives, which in every society submitted to our experience, impel human conduct in various directions. For the solution of the present enquiry, however, it is indispensably requisite to detach from this confused assemblage the inducement of natural religion, and to measure the force of the impulse which they communicate.

There are two modes of determining this point. 1. By analysing the nature and properties of these superhuman inducements, and comparing them with those human motives which commonly actuate our conduct. We shall thus discover how far those elements, which constitute and measure the force and efficiency of all human expectations, are to be found in the superhuman. 2. By examining those cases where accident places them in a state of single and unassisted agency, and thus fortifying the preceding analysis with the direct certificate of experience, so far as that is attainable.

Before, however, we embark in this investigation, it will be important to examine in what degree the superhuman expectations, supposing their influence purely beneficial, can be considered as indispensable instruments in the production of happiness in this life; or in other words, what is the number and importance of those cases, in which human inducements would be inapplicable and inoperative, and in which posthumous expectations would effectually supply the defect.

It will be easy to see that such cases are comparatively neither numerous nor important. For wherever the legislator can distinguish what actions it is desirable either to encourage or to prevent, he can always annex to them a measure of temporal reward or punishment commensurate to the purpose. It is only necessary that he should be able to distinguish and define such actions. To affirm therefore the necessity of a recurrence to superhuman agency for the repression of any definable mode of conduct, is merely to say that human laws are defective and require amendment. If this be true, let them be amended, and there will remain no ground for the complaint.

The gradations (you urge) by which guilt passes into innocence are often so nice as to be undiscoverable by the human eye, and to require the searching gaze of Omnipotence to detect their real point of separation. But if this be the case, how is it possible for the agent himself to know when he is acting well, and when he is verging towards evil? The two are undistinguishable to all men besides; why should they be otherwise to him? He knows his own intention, indeed, perfectly: It is to perform a certain action, of which no one can tell whether the tendency is beneficial or injurious. He himself cannot tell either; It is possible that he may suspect the action to be mischievous, and still intend to commit it. But he may be in error on this point, even after the most accurate consideration, and where the distinction between good and evil is so completely unassignable, the chances of error are as great as those of truth. Expectation of punishment, in case of wrong decision, could only render him more attentive in weighing the consequences, and even after this, it appears, he would be just as likely to decide wrong as right. Consequently the expectation of punishment produces no benefit whatever. Besides, if he can judge correctly, the foundations of such a judgment may be comprehended, and the offence defined, by the legislator. In all cases therefore in which guilt cannot be defined, and thence, no punishment awarded by the legislator, the apprehension of punishment from any foreign source is unproductive of any advantage.

But there are cases in which an individual may commit an act expressly forbidden by the law, relying on the impossibility or difficulty of detection. Doubtless there are such: And it is impossible to deny that on those occasions the apprehension of a posthumous verdict, from which there was no escape, *might possibly* supply an unavoidable defect in the reach of human laws. Secret crimes, however, are the only cases in which the superhuman inducements can be pretended to effect an end to which human motives would be inadequate. In all other occasions, the inefficacy of human laws is merely a reproach to the legislator, who neglects to remedy a known defect. And even in the case of hidden delinquency, how frequently is the escape of the criminal owing to mistakes perfectly corrigible, such as an unskilful police, exclusion of evidence, barbarity in the punishment awarded, and other circumstances which tend to unnerve the arm of the law! Supposing these imperfections to be removed,—suppose the penal code to be comprehensive and methodical, and its execution cheap, speedy, and vigilant, it would scarcely be practicable for the criminal to escape detection, when it was known that the crime had been committed.

It is only, therefore, when a crime is known, and the criminal undiscoverable, that superhuman inducements can be vindicated as indispensibly necessary for the maintenance of good conduct. And as these cases must, under a well-contrived system, be uncommonly rare, the necessity and importance of such inducements must be restricted within very narrow limits.

This is a point of some consequence. For if it should appear that these posthumous expectations are on many occasions of injurious tendency, the immediate inquiry must be, what exclusive benefit this mode of operating upon human conduct presents, in preference to any other. In reply to which, we have just demonstrated, that those cases in which beneficial influence is derivable solely from this source and not from any other, are few and inconsiderable. The extent of evil in this life would therefore be trifling, were superhuman inducements entirely effaced from the human bosom, and earthly institutions ameliorated according to the progress of philosophy. The pernicious tendency, which the former manifest on many occasions, will thus be compensated only by a very slender portion of essential and exclusive benefit.

These considerations also evince, that if it were practicable to supply the defect of human restrictions by recourse to a foreign world, we should be anxious to import active and faithful informers—to purchase such a revelation as would render our inferences of criminality more easy, precise, and extensive, in order that guilt might never escape our detection. We should not desire to introduce instruments for multiplying and protracting human torture. With these we are abundantly provided, if it were prudent or desirable to employ them. No earthly legislator, therefore, would attempt, if in his power, to perfect the efficacy of temporal enactments in the mode by which it is pretended that posthumous expectations accomplish this beneficial end.

CHAPTER VI

Efficiency of superhuman Inducements to produce temporal Evil. Their inefficiency to produce temporal Good.

Since it has been shewn in a former chapter that the directive rule, to which the inducements of natural religion attach themselves, will infallibly be detrimental to human happiness, it follows of course that these inducements, if they produce any effect at all, must be efficient to a mischievous purpose. I now propose to investigate the extent of influence which they exercise over mankind, as well as the manner of their operation.

All inducements are expectations either of pleasure or pain. The force with which all expectations act upon the human bosom varies according as they differ in, 1. Intensity,—2. Duration,—3. Certainty,—4. Propinquity. These are the four elements of value which constitute and measure the comparative strength of all human motives.

Take for example an expected pleasure. What are the motives which govern a man in the investment of money? He prefers that mode in which the profits are largest, most certain, and quickest. Present to him a speculation of greater hazard or in which he must be kept longer out of his money; the value of such an expectation is less, and he will not embrace it unless allured by a larger profit. Deficiency in certainty and propinquity will thus be compensated by an increase of intensity and duration.

To appreciate, therefore, the sway which posthumous expectations exercise over the behaviour of mankind, we must examine to what degree they comprise these elements of value.

First, they are to the highest degree deficient in *propinquity*. Every one conceives them as extremely remote; and in the greatest number of instances, such remoteness is conformable to experience, as insurance calculations testify.

Secondly, they are also defective in *certainty*. Posthumous pleasures and pains are reserved to be awarded in the lump, after a series of years. The only possible mode of distributing them, at such a period must be by reviewing the whole life of the individual—by computing his meritorious and culpable acts and striking a balance between them. It is impossible to conceive an expectation more deplorably uncertain, than that which such a scale of award must generate. In order to strip it of this character of doubt, the individual should have kept an exact journal of his debtor and creditor account with regard to post-obituary dispensations. Who ever does or ever did this? Yet if it is not done, so universal is self-deceit, that every man will unquestionably over-estimate his own extent of observance. His impression will thus be, that he has a balance in hand, and that the performance of any particular forbidden act will but slightly lessen the ample remainder which awaits him. But suppose it otherwise—let him imagine that the balance is against him. There still remains the chance of future amendment and compensation, by which it may be rendered favourable, and this prospect is incalculably more liable to exaggeration than the estimate which he forms of his past conduct.

The prodigious excess to which mankind heap up splendid purposes for the coming year, is matter of notoriety and even of ridicule. A slight accession of punishment incurred by what the individual may be about to do at the moment, will be lost in the contemplation of the mass of subsequent reward. Posthumous expectations must, therefore, under every supposition, be pre-eminently defective in the element of certainty.

To make up for this want of certainty and propinquity, the pleasures and pains anticipated in a future life are (it will be urged) intense and durable to the utmost extent. Imagination, no doubt, (our sole guide under unassisted natural religion) may magnify and protract them beyond all limit, since there is no direct testimony which can check her career. But it should be remarked that this excessive intensity and permanence can never be otherwise than purely imaginary, nor can the most appalling descriptions of fancy ever impart to them that steady and equable impressiveness which characterises a real scene subjected to the senses. As all our ideas of pleasure and pain are borrowed from experience, the most vivid anticipations we can frame cannot possibly surpass the liveliest sensation. Magnify the intensity as you will, this must be its ultimate boundary. But you never can stretch it even so high as this point: For to do this would be to exalt the conceptions of fancy to a level with real and actual experience, so that the former shall affect the mind as vividly as the latter—which is the sole characteristic of insanity, and the single warrant for depriving the unhappy madman of his liberty.

If, indeed, the expectations actually created in the mind corresponded in appalling effect to the descriptions of the fancy—and if the defects of certainty and propinquity could be so far counteracted as to leave these expectations in full possession of the mind—the result must be, absolute privation of reason, and an entire sacrifice of all sublunary enjoyment. The path of life must lie as it were on the brink of a terrific precipice, where it would be impossible to preserve a sound and distinct vision, and where the imminent and inextricable peril of our situation would altogether absorb the mind, so as to leave us no opportunity for building up any associations of comfort or delight. A man who is to have an operation performed in a short space of time, cannot dismiss it from his thoughts for an instant; How much less, if he sees, or believes that he sees, a gigantic hand, armed with instruments of exquisite torture, and menacing his defenceless frame?

Such must be the result, if these anticipations did really affect the mind, in a degree proportional to their imagined intensity. They cannot be conceived as tolerably near and certain, without driving the believer mad, and without rendering it a far more desireable lot for him to have had no life at all, than the two lives taken together. Looking therefore to the happiness of the present life alone, it appears to be merely saved from complete annihilation, by that diminished influence of the posthumous prospects which distance and uncertainty cannot fail to occasion. It is their inefficiency, and not their efficiency, which constitutes the safeguard of human comfort.

But what is the real value of this residuary influence? To determine this question, we must consult the analogy of human conduct and observe the effect of large expectations, when remote and uncertain, as compared with others of small amount, but close at hand and specific.

How painful are the apprehensions which the approach of death creates? To preserve the mind from being altogether overpowered by them, and to maintain a cool deportment at such an instant, is supposed to be an effort of more than human firmness. Thus terrible and overwhelming is the prospect when merely approximated to the eye. Strip it of its propinquity, and all its effect upon the mind immediately vanishes. Its real terrors, its ultimate certainty, remain unimpaired; but delay the moment, for a few years at farthest, and the whole scene is immediately dismissed from the thoughts. So confident and neglectful do we become upon the subject, that it requires more than ordinary forethought to make those provisions which a due regard to the happiness of our survivors would enjoin.

This is an illustration of peculiar value, because it is a case in which mere remoteness practically annuls the most dreadful of all expectations, without insinuating even the most transient suspicion of ultimate escape. But if distance alone will produce so striking a deduction, how much will its negative effect be heightened, when coupled with uncertainty as to the eventful fulfilment? It seems apparent that these two negative circumstances, taken together, must altogether prevent the most painful anticipations from ever affecting the mind, unless under very peculiar circumstances, which we shall presently notice.[2]

Analogy therefore seems to testify most indisputably, that sufferings so remote and so uncertain as those of a posthumous life, whatever may be their fancied intensity, can scarcely affect the mind at all, in its natural state. Such anticipations can only obtain

---

2. This important principle, that a small amount of pain, if quick and certain in its application, provides a more effectual restraint than the most painful death, when delay and the chance of complete escape is interposed—seems to be pretty generally recognized at the present day. Instruments of torture have consequently become obsolete; and most of the alterations of the legislator have been designed to cure the lame foot, and to accelerate the pace of justice. In this, indeed, his aim has been not merely to prevent in the most complete manner the commission of crime, but also to prevent it at the expence of the smallest possible aggregate of suffering. For to denounce penalties of shocking severity, but tardy and uncertain in their execution, would be to create the greatest sum of artificial pain, with the least possible preventive effect. This would be entirely at variance with the genuine spirit of legislation, whose end is the extension of human happiness by the eradication of noxious acts. This, however, cannot be the purpose of the God of natural religion; who is uniformly conceived (as I have before remarked) to delight in human misery, and who is therefore supposed, with perfect consistency, to inflict pain where the pain itself cannot produce a particle of benefit, and where the anticipation of it can have no effect whatever in repressing vicious conduct.

possession of it when introduced by other analogous ideas, which have previously perverted the usual current of thought, and rendered it fit for their reception. Under such circumstances, these new allies cannot fail to aggravate most powerfully that tone of sentiment to which they owe their origin. Their distance and uncertainty will be forgotten, and they will be conceived as imminent and inevitable; while the impression of their intensity will be more vehement than ever. Such will be the case in the peculiar state of mind to which we here allude; But taking mankind as they usually think and judge, it is altogether contrary to experience that posthumous expectations should ever be otherwise than nugatory.

Now if, according to the general tenor of thought, they become thus dormant and inoperative, they cannot possibly be employed as restraints upon crime. For when crime is committed, the mind is under the sway of a present and actuating temptation. It is not only exempt from all such associations as might contribute to kindle up the thoughts of posthumous terrors; but it is under the strong grasp and impulse of a contrary passion, which fills it with ideas of a totally opposite character. So completely indeed does the temptation absorb the whole soul, that it is difficult in many cases to counteract it by the most immediate and unequivocal prospect of impending evil. But unless the punishment denounced obtrudes itself upon the delinquent with a force sufficiently pressing and inflexible to overbear the sophistry of temptation, we may be assured that he will be insensible to the threats and will commit the crime. How much more then, where the apprehended evil is so remote and uncertain, and the value of the expectation so fluctuating and occasional, as to require a peculiarly favourable tone of thought before the mind can be induced to harbour it? We are surely authorised in deeming an expectation so constituted altogether useless as a motive to resist any strong desire.

But what is that preliminary state of mind into which posthumous apprehensions find so easy an admittance? It is that in which congenial feelings have been predominant—a state of timidity and depression, when gloomy associations overspread the whole man, and cast horror and wretchedness round his future prospects. In this condition, the fountains of all painful thought are opened, and posthumous terrors present an inexhaustible fund of kindred matter. Their distance and their uncertainty are of no consequence, for the mensuration of the mental eye is at such a period confounded, and it distinguishes not the scene before it. Their indeterminate character renders them only the more appropriate, for the imagination demands but a plausible pretence and outline, to conjure up the amplest detail of terrific particulars. In sickness and in nervous despondency, associations of this kind make their most disastrous inroads, and contribute most actively to plunge the mind into that state of unassuageable terror, which borders so closely on insanity, and frequently terminates in it. And in the hour of death, when these apprehensions seem on the brink of reality, they obtrude themselves in thick and appalling clouds, and aggravate that prostration both of bodily and mental faculties, which marks the close of existence.

Such is the force, and such the mode of operation, belonging to these superhuman expectations, when acting singly. And it appears from hence most undeniably, that they are almost wholly inefficient on every occasion when it might have been possible for them to enlarge the sum of temporal happiness—and efficient only in cases where they swell the amount of temporal misery.

For the only benefit which they are calculated to accomplish would be the repression of crimes. To this purpose it has been shewn that they are wholly inadequate; for during the influence of temptation, the only season in which a man commits crime, they find no place in the mind, and therefore can interpose no barrier. On the other hand, they act with the highest effect at a period when they cannot by possibility produce any temporal benefit—that is, at the close of life: and the extent of their influence is always in an inverse ratio to the demand for it. The greater the previous despondency, the wider the space which they occupy, and the more powerfully do they contribute to heighten those morbid associations which the overmastered reason is unable to dispel.

CHAPTER VII

Analysis of the source from whence the real Efficiency of superhuman Enjoyments is almost wholly derived.

Since the inducements which we have been discussing are altogether impotent as a barrier to temptation, and influential only in peculiar states of mind, how happens it (we may be asked) that their dominion in human affairs should be apparently so extensive? The cause of this seeming contrariety, which merely arises from a misconception regarding the actual motives of mankind, I shall now endeavour to unfold.

It has already been shewn that the God of natural religion is uniformly conceived as delighting in the contemplation of his own superiority and in the receipt of human obedience—that is, in the debasement, the privations, and the misery of mankind. Now each man has a strong temptation to elude any payment,[3] in his own person, of these unpleasant burthens; but he has no temptation what-

3. The Reverend Mr. Colton, (in a collection of thoughts entitled "Lacon"—Vol. 1. XXV.) says, "Men will wrangle for religion; write for it; fight for it; die for it; *any thing but—live* for it." The same divine also asserts, in the same volume, CLXXXIX. "Where true religion has prevented one crime, false religions have afforded a pretext for a thousand." There cannot be a stronger acknowledgement of the enormous balance of temporal evil, which religion, considered on the whole, inflicts on mankind.

ever to avert from others the necessity of paying them. On the contrary, a powerful interest inclines him to exert himself in strictly exacting from every other man the requisite quota. For the Deity, pleased with human obedience, will of course be pleased with those faithful allies who aid him in obtaining it, and will in consideration of this assistance be more indulgent towards themselves. Each man, therefore, anxious for the lighter and more profitable service, will take part with God, and will volunteer his efforts to enforce upon all other men that line of conduct most agreeable to the divine Being. This spontaneous zeal in extorting payment from his brother debtors will dispose the creditor to remit or to alleviate his own debt.

But each individual will also be perfectly conscious that these temptations are equally active in the bosoms of his neighbors. They also are upon the watch to recommend themselves to God by avenging his insulted name, and obviating any interruptions to the leisure and satisfaction of Omnipotence. They readily bring forward their terrestrial reinforcements—abuse, hatred, and injury, against any individual who forswears his allegiance to the unseen sovereign—eulogy and veneration towards him who renders it with more than ordinary strictness. Each man is thus placed under the surveillance of the rest. A strong public antipathy is pointed against impious conduct; the decided approbation of the popular voice is secured in favour of religious acts. The praise or blame of his earthly companions, will thus become the real actuating motive to religious observances on the part of each individual. By an opposite conduct it is not merely the divine denunciations that he provokes, but also the hostility of innumerable crusaders, who long to expiate their own debts by implacable warfare against the recusant.

But although thus in fact determined to a pious behaviour by the esteem and censure of his fellows, he will have the highest interest in disguising this actual motive, and in pretending to be influenced only by genuine veneration for the being whom he worships. A religious act, if performed from any other than a religious feeling, loses its character of exclusive reference to the Deity, and of course ceases to be agreeable to him. But if God is no longer satisfied with this semi-voluntary performance of the service required, neither will the neighbourhood, who take up arms in God's favour, be satisfied with it. No individual, therefore, will be able to steer clear of the public enmity, unless he not only renders these pious acts of homage, but also succeeds in convincing others that he is actuated in rendering them entirely by the fear of God. The popular sanction, therefore, not only enforces the delivery of the homage; It also compels the deliverer to carry all the marks of being influenced solely by religious inducements, and to pretend that he would act precisely in the same manner, whatever might be the sentiments of his neighbours.

The same pretence too will be encouraged by other considerations. When a man is once compelled by some extraneous motive to go through the service, it will be his interest to claim all that merit in the eyes of God which a spontaneous performance of it would have insured. He will, therefore, assume all the exterior mien of a voluntary subjection to the invisible Being, and will endeavour to deceive himself into a belief that this is his genuine motive. In this self-imposition he will most commonly succeed, and his account of his own conduct, originally insincere, will in time be converted into unconscious and unintentional error.

We can now interpret this seeming contrariety between the natural impotence and the alleged apparent dominion, of religious inducements. For the real fact is, that they enlist in their service the irresistible arm of public opinion—and that too in a manner which secures to themselves all the credit of swaying mankind, while the actually determining motive is by general consent suppressed and kept out of view.

Religion is thus enabled to apply, for the encouragement and discouragement of those acts which fall within her sphere, the very same engines as morality. Moral conduct springs from the mutual wants and interests of mankind. It is each man's interest that his neighbour should be virtuous; Hence each man knows, that the public opinion will approve his conduct, if virtuous—reprobate it, if vicious. Religious acts, indeed, no man has any motive to approve from any benefit conferred by the actual performance of them; or, to disapprove the opposite behaviour from any injury referable to it. But every man has something to gain by being active in enforcing upon others the performance of these acts—inasmuch as this is a co-operation with the views of God, which may have the effect of partially discharging, or at least of lightening, his own obligations. The same encouragements and prohibition, therefore, which mankind apply to virtue and to vice, they will be led to annex, though from a totally opposite motive, to pious or impious behaviour.

When the public opinion has once occasioned, as it cannot fail to do, a tolerably extensive diffusion of religious practices throughout the community, the censures directed against any small remainder of nonconformists will be embittered by the concurrent action of envy. I feel myself constrained to be rigidly exact in the renewal of my pious offerings: Shall my neighbour, who eludes all share in the burthen and will not deduct a moment from his favourite pursuits for similar purposes, be treated with the same courtesy and respect as myself, who expend so much self-denial in order to ensure it? Is not the labourer worthy of his hire? Being myself a scrupulous renderer of these services, it becomes my interest, even with my fellow-countrymen, to swell the merit of performing them, and the criminality of neglect, to the highest possible pitch, in order to create a proportionate distribution of their esteem. The more deeply I can impress this conviction upon mankind, the greater will be their veneration for me. All these principles conspire to sharpen my acrimony against my non-conforming neighbour, and render me doubly dissatisfied with that state of respite and impunity in which Omnipotence still permits him to live. In this condition of mind, nothing can be more gratifying than the self-assumed task of executing the divine wrath upon his predestined head.

CHAPTER VIII

Proof of the Inefficiency of superhuman Inducements, when unassisted by, or at variance with, public Opinion.

By the preceding analysis I have attempted to shew, that the apparent influence of posthumous expectations is at the bottom nothing more than a disguised and peculiar agency of public opinion; and also to trace the process by which these expectations naturally and infallibly give birth to such an inflexion of the popular voice. I now propose to confirm this explanation still farther, by citing a few most convincing examples of the complete disregard with which posthumous anticipations are treated, when the voice of the public either opposes, or ceases to enforce, their influence.

For this purpose it will be absolutely necessary to allege instances from revealed religion, because it is only by means of revelation that a written, unvarying collection of precepts has become promulgated, completely independent of any variations which may take place in the national feeling. In natural religion it is impossible to discover what is the course of action enjoined, except by consulting the reigning tone of practice and sentiment;

and, therefore, the two must necessarily appear harmonious and coincident, since we can only infer the former from the latter. Revelation alone communicates a known and authoritative code, with which the actual conduct of believers may be compared, and the points of conformity or separation ascertained.

1. The first practice which may be cited, as manifesting the impotence of religious precepts, when opposed to public opinion, is that of duelling. Nothing can be more notoriously contrary to the divine law; which acts too on this occasion with every possible advantage, except the alliance of the popular voice. For the practice which religion here interdicts is attended with pain and hazard to the person committing it, and often with the most ruinous consequences to his surviving relatives. If ever superhuman inducements could ensure obedience when opposed to the popular sanction, it would be in a case where all other motives conspire to aid them.

If posthumous enjoyments were the actual reward aimed at, and the real motive for religious conduct, this concurrence of other inducements would swell their influence and render them preponderant. But the truth is, that they are not the actual reward sought by the religionist. What he desires is, *to prove to the satisfaction of other men that they are so*—to acquire in their eyes the credit of unbounded attachment to the Deity. No man will give him credit for any such attachment, simply because he declines a duel. He knows that the world will ascribe his refusal to cowardice—and thus the concurrence of motives abates and enfeebles, instead of confirming, the efficacy of the religious precept. He will be more ready to inflict upon himself severe bodily sufferings, in compliance with the divine code, than to follow its precepts where mankind will give him no credit for the sincerity of his obedience.

Whether, however, the justice of this solution be admitted or denied, the instance of duelling must in either case demonstrate the inefficiency of religious inducements, when opposed to public opinion.

2. *Fornication* is an act directly forbidden by the superhuman code—but not forbidden by the popular voice. The latter, however, does not in this case imperatively demand the infringement of the prohibitory precept, as it did in the case of the duel; but merely leaves the divine admonition to operate unsupported. To what extent it operates thus single-handed, the state of all great cities notoriously attests.

3. *Simony*, again, is forbidden in the religious code with equal strictness, and practised with equal frequency.

4. But perhaps the case in which the impotence of posthumous apprehensions is most glaring and manifest, is that of *perjury*. The person who takes an oath solemnly calls down upon himself the largest measure of divine vengeance, if he commits a particular act. In this imprecation it is implied, that he firmly anticipates the infliction of these penalties, if he becomes guilty of this self-condemned behaviour. Yet this expectation, which he thus attests and promulgates, of posthumous inflictions, has not, when stript of the consentient impulse of public opinion, the slenderest hold upon his actions. It cannot make him forego any temptation, however small; as an appeal to unexceptionable facts will evince.

Every young man, who is entered at the University of Oxford, is obliged to take an oath, that he will observe the statutes of the University—a collection of rules for his conduct while he is a student, framed many years ago by Archbishop Laud. On this oath, after it has been once taken, not a thought is bestowed, even by the most scrupulous religionist. Its precepts are altogether unheeded and forgotten—infringed of course on every occasion when the observance of them is at all inconvenient. The conduct of all the swearers is precisely the same as it would have been had the oath never been taken. All the posthumous vengeance which they have imprecated upon themselves—all the superhuman inflictions which they firmly anticipate—suffice not to produce the most trivial alteration of behaviour. Yet an adherence to some at least among the injunctions thus solemnly sealed, would entail scarcely any inconvenience at all. Slight, however, as this inconvenience is, the fear of post obituary penalties is still slighter, and, therefore, even the easy means of averting them are altogether neglected.

The regulations prescribed by the oath, it will be said, are useless, and, therefore, there is no necessity for observing them. This may be very true, and may afford an unanswerable reason for discontinuing the form altogether: But it offers not the shadow of a plea for neglecting its dictates, when you have once gone through the ceremonial. By virtue of the oath you have imposed upon yourself a special obligation to the performance of certain acts; You bind yourself by your apprehension of posthumous visitations in case of failure, and in order to obviate all reluctance on the part of the Almighty, you state your own fervent desire to be so treated. Whatever obligatory force was comprised in the formula, can never be impaired by your discovery that the act enjoined will produce no beneficial consequence.

The uselessness of these regulations is, indeed, the real cause why the oath to fulfil them remains universally unobserved. But why? Because the popular voice has no longer any interest in enforcing them. But the strength of the posthumous fears remains unaltered—and the result attests most strikingly *their* debility and nothingness.

As another confirmation of this doctrine, let us remark the conduct of Jurors, when they administer a law which popular opinion, as well as they themselves, condemn as sanguinary and impolitic. How undisguised is the manner in which they infringe their oaths in order to elude the necessity of passing a capital sentence! In defiance of the most irresistible testimony, they find a man guilty of stealing under the value of forty shillings, and thus consign him to the milder and more appropriate punishment. Whence comes it that the force of the oath, weighty and inflexible up to this point, suddenly dissolves into nothing and is shorn of all its credit? It is because the popular voice has ceased to uphold it. Public opinion gave, and public opinion has taken away; and all the sway, which superhuman expectations possess over human behaviour, is surreptitiously procured, from their coincidence with this omnipotent sanction.

Though it is popular opinion, or the desire of temporal esteem, which forms the actuating stimulus to religious observances, yet there are unquestionably instances in which such works have been faithfully performed without any prospect of consequent credit—nay, perhaps, in spite of bitter and predominant enmity. This is perfectly conformable to the general analogy of nature. For when the associations of credit have once linked themselves with any course of behaviour, by conversation with a peculiar class, by strong personal affection, or any other cause—when the feeling of self-respect has become attached to that course—an individual will not unfrequently persevere in it, though the harvest which he reaps may not actually gratify and realize the association. What is the motive which impels the friends of mankind to exert themselves in reforming a bad government? It springs unquestionably from the desire of esteem; first the desire of obtaining it, then that of deserving it, whether it is actually attainable or not. A similar anxiety, for veneration and influence over the sentiments of others, possesses the religionist, even when he both anticipates and encounters unqualified obloquy; and the fury of proselytism, which is inseparable from his tone of feeling, attests this beyond all dispute. Even the solitary penance of the monk springs from the very same principle; for the association of credit, when once deeply implanted, will govern human conduct, though there should be no prospect of realizing the hope which originally engendered it.

In addition to this it should be remarked, that no one can question the powerful influence exercised by superhuman inducements, in some peculiar cases. They sometimes produce insanity. But these are exceptions to their usual impotence, and cannot be admitted as evidence against the general conclusion which we have just established.

As it has been demonstrated that all the efficacy of posthumous inducements is in reality referable to their alliance with public opinion—we at once discover the weakness of that plea by which these inducements were asserted to affect secret crimes, uncognizable by human laws. He who entertains confident hopes of perpetrating a misdeed without detection, will of course pay no regard to the popular voice. Nor will the fear of future pains, stripped of that auxiliary which alone renders it formidable, counteract a temptation to delinquency, when we see that it cannot prevail upon an Oxford student to undergo the smallest inconvenience. That the conduct of the former is guilty and injurious—the neglect of the latter, innocent—is a distinction which does not in the least vitiate the analogy. They are both under the special and solitary restraint, whatever be its power, which superhuman terrors impose. The one therefore may serve as an unexceptionable measure of the other. Nay, if any thing, these fears ought to be more potent and effective in the case of the Oxford student, than in that of the secret criminal—inasmuch as the former has himself solicited and sanctioned their infliction, and has originated his own claim for their fulfilment.

But if posthumous apprehensions are inapplicable for the coercion of secret crime, it cannot be pretended that they are ever necessary—for human enactments will embrace all open and definable delinquency. To say that earthly laws do not actually perform this, is merely to affirm, that governments are defective and ought to be reformed.

RECAPITULATION

The foregoing search into the nature and action of those posthumous expectations which unassisted natural religion furnishes, has envinced, I trust conclusively: 1. That in the absence of any authorised directive rule, the class of actions which our best founded inference would suggest as entitling the performer to post-obituary reward, is one not merely useless, but strikingly detrimental, to mankind in the present life; while the class conceived as meriting future punishment, is one always innocuous, often beneficial, to our fellow creatures on earth. 2. That from the character and properties of posthumous inducements, they infallibly become impotent for the purpose of resisting any temptation whatever, and efficient only in the production of needless and unprofitable misery. 3. That the influence exercised by these inducements is, in most cases, really derived from the popular sanction, which they are enabled to bias and enlist in their favour.

If these conclusions are correct, I think it cannot be denied, that the influence possessed by natural religion over human conduct is, with reference to the present life, injurious to an extent incalculably greater than it is beneficial. For if it ever does produce benefit, this must be owing to casual and peculiar associations in the minds of some few believers, who form an exception to the larger body. It is by no means my design to question the existence of some persons thus happily born or endowed. But it would be most unsafe and perilous to build our general doctrine on a few such instances of rare merit. We can only determine the general operation of these inducements, or the effect which they produce on the greatest number of minds, by analysing their nature and properties, and by contemplating the result which these properties bring about in other known cases. This is what has been here attempted, and the inquiry has demonstrated that the agency of superhuman motives must in the larger aggregate of instances, produce effects decidedly pernicious to earthly happiness.

Having thus ascertained that the general influence of unaided natural religion is mischievous, with reference to the present life, I shall now proceed to expose the mischief more in detail,—to particularize and classify its various forms.

PART II

Catalogue of the various modes in which natural religion is mischievous.

In enumerating the various modes in which posthumous expectations, when unaided by revelation, are productive of injury, it will be expedient to classify them under two heads:

1. Mischiefs accruing to an individual, separately considered.
2. Mischiefs not merely self-affecting, but contagious—diffusing themselves more or less widely throughout the society.

CHAPTER I

Of the mischiefs accruing to the Individual.

MISCHIEF I—INFLICTING UNPROFITABLE SUFFERING.

There is an interminable variety in the particularities which characterize natural religion, amongst different nations of the globe. But its genuine spirit and tone is throughout the same, yesterday, to-day, and for ever. The same motive pervades all its votaries, whether in Hindostan or Mexico; and though it may impel them with greater strength and sovereignty in one climate or age, than in another, yet there is not the smallest difficulty in tracing its identity every where.

You wish to give proof of your attachment to the Deity, in the eyes and for the conviction of your fellow-men? There is but one species of testimony which will satisfy their minds. You must impose upon yourself pain for his sake; and in order to silence all suspicion as to the nature of the motive, the pain must be such as not to present the remotest prospect of any independent reward. I have already attempted to shew, that this condition effectually excludes, and renders improper for the purpose, all suffering endured for the benefit of mankind. Mankind will measure your devotion to God by the amount and intensity of the pain which you thus gratuitously inflict upon yourself. Accordingly we see, that wherever the religious principle has been most predominant, and the counteracting hand of reason the most feeble, the mass of torture thus voluntarily imposed has been the most deplorable, revolting, and unprofitable.

Almost all the modes of pain, both physical and mental, seem to have been selected at different places and periods, for the purpose of demonstrating the magnitude and sincerity of the extra-human affections.

MISCHIEF II—IMPOSING USELESS PRIVATIONS.

It is by endurance of voluntary pain that a man can most invincibly attest his devotion to the Deity. But there seems to have been a gradual declension of genuine and fervid piety in many countries, or at least its intensity has frequently fallen short of this first-rate excellence. In this state of comparative relaxation, it suffices only to enforce upon its votaries the greater or less immolation of earthly pleasures, without being strong enough to produce gratuitous self-torture. Public opinion, less impassioned and less exciteable on behalf of the Deity, will not reimburse the sufferer for the endurance of stripes and mutilation. The motive to the latter being thus withdrawn, he contents himself with colder and more moderate testimonies of devotion. He claims the public esteem for a voluntary resignation of all his earthly pleasures for the sake of God. To impress this conviction in the minds of his neighbours, it is necessary that his self-denial should be above all imputation of temporal recompence—and therefore that it should be productive of little or no benefit to any beside the Deity.

Of all the sources of pleasure, physical and mental, few can be named which have not thus become, in a greater or less degree, objects of renunciation and abhorrence. The following acts of self-denial have all, on different occasions, been placed in the catalogue of religious practices:

1. Fasting.
2. Celibacy.
3. Abstinence from repose.
4. Abstinence from cleanliness, personal decoration, and innocent comforts.
5. Abstinence from social enjoyments and mirth.
6. Abstinence from remedies to disease.
7. Gratuitous surrender of property, time and labour.
8. Surrender of dignity and honours.

It is unnecessary to remark that none of these privations inflict that acute and immediate agony, which results from the tortures before enumerated. Some of them, perhaps, may upon the long run occasion a larger aggregate of suffering, from their constant pressure and irritation. But I think it most important to notice, that out of the whole diminution of human happiness, which natural religion originates, these intense self-inflictions constitute a portion almost infinitely small, when compared with that spreading system of privation and self-denial, which lays whole societies under contribution. Like a vicious government, the amount of its noxious effects ought to be estimated by the standing sacrifices which it extorts from the million, and which, though not strikingly oppressive in any individual case, swell into an unfathomable mass when multiplied into the countless host upon whom they are levied—not from the comparatively rare occurrences of concentrated horror and atrocity.

For public opinion, which merely encourages and provokes, by excessive admiration, the voluntary tortures of the enthusiast, acts as a compulsory force in extorting self-denial and asceticism. How it originally comes to demand and enforce these sacrifices, how each individual finds himself interested in exacting them from others, and thence obliged to pay them himself—I have attempted to elucidate in the foregoing part. The reason why the privations are thus required by the popular voice, while the self-inflictions are left optional, is because the earliest and most natural mode which occurs for conciliating the unseen misanthrope, is to consign to his use some gratifying and valuable possession. A man despoils himself of some piece of property, and bestows it to satisfy the wants of his Deity: The Ostiak, according to Pallas, takes a quantity of meat and places it between the lips of his idol—other nations present drink to the Gods by throwing it out of the cup upon the ground; that is, by rendering it useless to any human being. It is these donatives, or acts of privation, which are originally conceived as recommending the performer to divine favour. Sacrifices of other sorts are subsequently super-added—and abstinences from certain enjoyments, on the plea of consecrating them to the Deity. Hence the public opinion is at the outset warmly enlisted in exacting self-denying performances for his benefit—a tone of thought industriously cherished by his ministers, as I shall hereafter explain.[4]

These considerations will serve to explain how the popular

4. Self imposed torture seems to be a subsequent refinement, devised by poor men who had no property to make donations, and whose time cannot be spared from the task of providing subsistence. In order to gain a living, as well as to make good his claim to the public admiration, the naked enthusiast must give manifestations of internal feeling which may strike the beholder with awe. But utter destitution admits of no farther self-denial, and can elevate itself above others only by insensibility to pain, which appears to place it beyond the reach of human menaces. Hence the incredible sufferings which have been voluntarily endured by monks and fakirs, and the prodigious veneration which, among ignorant nations, they have seldom failed to inspire—a veneration which has doubtless on some occasions caused them to be practised even by the rich.

opinion has come to compel imperiously a certain measure of self-denial and privation, while it abandons self-inflicted penance to the kindlings of spontaneous enthusiasm.

MISCHIEF III—IMPRESSING UNDEFINED TERRORS.

In treating generally of the efficacy of these posthumous anticipations in the character of sanctions, I have already indicated the mode in which they kindle up, on certain occasions, the most terrific feelings of which the human bosom is susceptible. Their operation is indeed most afflicting, in this point of view; it is always most cruelly preponderant upon those unhappy subjects whose title to exemption is the greatest—upon those who are already broken down by sickness and despondency—upon those whose only point of distinction from their neighbours is the actual calamity under which they suffer. This unfortunate casualty shatters the nervous system, enfeebles the judgment, and lays open the victim to the incursions of imaginary terrors, the extent and reality of which he cannot measure. The force, which religion thus casts into the already over-poised scale of misery, may be best appreciated by stating, that it frequently drives the sufferer into insanity. It augments also most fatally the horrors which usually environ the prospect of death.

But I need not again repeat what has been before urged, that these anticipations redouble their severity precisely at the time when no benefit can possibly result from it. They slumber during the period of health and comfort; they await the appearance of sorrow and disaster before they can obtain a congenial atmosphere. The mass of suffering which they thus occasion to almost every one, at different times of life, must be very considerable. There is no one who has not been occasionally assailed by illness, and by the despondency which generally attends it, and few, therefore, into whose mind posthumous fears do not at times find admission, with more or less effect. We are warranted then in assuming the aggregate of misery introduced by them in this shape, as highly important in amount. That almost all persons, in whom religion is deeply and fervently implanted, are much harrassed by these distressing apprehensions, may be asserted with confidence. But it is seldom that we can obtain a testimony at once so striking and authentic, of their power and extent, as the following account of the Spanish monasteries—written by a philosophical Spanish clergyman, and contained in a most eloquent and interesting work entitled "Don Leucadio Doblado's Letters from Spain"—(London, 1822).

"The common source of suffering (says this author p. 252) among the Catholic recluses, proceeds from a certain degree of religious melancholy, which, combined with such complaints as originate in perpetual confinement, affect more or less the greater number. The mental disease to which I allude, is commonly known by the name of *Escrupulos*, and might be called *religious anxiety*. It is *the natural state of a mind perpetually dwelling on hopes connected with an invisible world*, and *anxiously practising means to avoid an unhappy lot in it, which keep the apprehended danger for ever present to the imagination*. Consecration for life at the altar promises, it is true, increased happiness in the world to come; but the numerous and difficult duties attached to the religious profession, multiply the hazards of eternal misery with the chances of failure in their performance, and while the plain Christian's offences against the moral law are often considered as mere frailties, those of the professed votary seldom escape the aggravation of sacrilege. The odious diligence of the Catholic moralists has raked together an endless catalogue of sins, by *thought, word, and deed*, to every one of which the punishment of eternal flames has been assigned. This list, alike horrible and disgusting, haunts the imagination of the unfortunate devotee, till reduced to a state of perpetual anxiety, she can neither think, speak, nor act, without discovering in every vital motion a sin which invalidates all her past sacrifices, and dooms her painful efforts after Christian perfection to end in everlasting misery. Absolution, which adds boldness to the resolute and profligate, becomes a fresh source of disquietude to a timid and sickly mind. Doubts innumerable disturb the unhappy sufferer, not however as to the power of the priest in granting pardon but respecting her own fulfilment of the conditions, without which to receive pardon is sacrilege. These *agonizing fears*, cherished and fed by the small circle of objects to which a nun is confined, *are generally incurable, and usually terminate in an untimely death or insanity.*"

MISCHIEF IV—TAXING PLEASURE, BY THE INFUSION OF PRELIMINARY SCRUPLES, AND SUBSEQUENT REMORSE.

Among the mischievous effects of religion in the present life, it is necessary to advert to those cases where the innocuous pleasure, which it proscribes, is still, in defiance of the mandate, enjoyed. In these circumstances its effect is not so great as absolutely to discard the pleasure, but only to damp and darken it; partly by introducing a previous doubt or opposition of motives; partly by obtruding, when the vehemence of the conquering passions has subsided, a mixture of shame and regret oftentimes insupportably bitter. Though religion thus does not entirely preclude our enjoyment, yet she compels us to purchase it by unhappiness both antecedent and consequent.

CHAPTER II

Of the Mischiefs which Natural Religion occasions, not only to the Believer himself, but also to others through his means.

MISCHIEF I—CREATING FACTITIOUS ANTIPATHY.

The preparation in the human bosom for antipathy towards other men is, under all circumstances, most unhappily copious and active. The boundless range of human desires, and the very limited number of objects adapted to satisfy them, unavoidably leads a man to consider those with whom he is obliged to share such objects, as inconvenient rivals who narrow his own extent of enjoyment. Besides, human beings are the most powerful instruments of production, and therefore every one becomes anxious to employ the services of his fellows in multiplying his own comforts. Hence the intense and universal thirst for power; the equally prevalent hatred of subjection. Each man therefore meets with an obstinate resistance to his own will, and is obliged to make an equally constant opposition to that of others, and this naturally engenders antipathy towards the beings who thus baffle and contravene his wishes.

Religion becomes a powerful coadjutor to these predisposing causes. Almost all her influence, as we have before explained, is derived from the system of rivalry and mutual compulsion which she introduces among mankind—each man recommending himself to the divine favour, by extorting from others the sacrifice of their inclinations on behalf of God. Hence arises an immense extension of the principle of antipathy; a number of factitious instances are created and subjected to its controul, where it had before no application; and every fresh case of collision swells and aggravates the ill-will which sprung from the previous sources.

Those artificial antipathies, which are the peculiar growth and fruit of religion, assume a variety of shapes, and ramify widely throughout the field of human actions. The principal circumstances on which they fasten are reducible to these three;

1. Unbelief in the existence of the Deity.
2. Non-observance of his will.
3. Mal-observance of his will.

1. Of all human antipathies, that which the believer in a God bears to the unbeliever is the fullest, the most unqualified, and the most universal. All considerations and feelings conspire to aggravate it; scarcely a thought suggests itself in mitigation of an offence so heinous. First, the mere circumstance of dissent, involving a tacit imputation of error and incapacity, and envincing that our persuasive power is not rated so highly by others as it is by ourselves, invariably begets dislike towards our antagonist. By attempting to demonstrate that we are in error, he robs us in part of our influence and credit with mankind, from which we should have reaped many advantages had our doctrines remained unchallenged. Secondly, the feeling of hostility which the believer entertains towards the unbeliever, on the score of dissent, in incalcula-

bly more acute than that which the latter generally imbibes against him. For an excessive and inconsiderate credulity is indicative of a far weaker cast of mind than over-caution and incredulity. The former lays its possessor open to unceasing miscalculation and deception: the latter is on numerous occasions an entire preservative—scarcely ever a cause of suffering or of loss. Hence to him who takes the negative side of a question, the believer in the affirmative is more the object of contempt than of hatred, being regarded as simple, uninquiring, and easily duped or misled. Ridicule is the weapon which the unbeliever is most disposed to employ. On the other hand, the believer knows perfectly the light of inferiority in which his antagonist views him: and to be considered by others as silly and contemptible, occasions the most poignant and intolerable vexation, since the diffusion of this sentiment would altogether bereave us of the attention and favour of mankind, which is never conferred on those who are too feeble to deserve or repay it. Now the unbeliever is of course interested, like every other man, in spreading his own opinions, and will attempt this whenever it is practicable. We need not wonder therefore, that the believer manifests the bitterest aversion towards one who is endeavouring to impress mankind with the meanest estimate of his judgment and penetration.

All the strong passions of humanity are thus let loose against the unbeliever, and coincide perfectly with our anxiety to vindicate the divine majesty, by protecting it from neglect or insult on the part of any one else. The antipathy therefore is in this case swelled to the utmost pitch of intensity, nor is there a single consideration which can tend to repress or mitigate it. It dictates and furnishes a pretence for the gratification of an existing wish: it requires no troublesome subjugation of propensities, no surrender of actual enjoyments. It does not pledge the believer to any painful observances, in order to ensure consistency between his sentiments and his conduct. He who neglects altogether the more costly modes of purchasing posthumous promotion, will be so much the more interested in magnifying the importance of belief and the heinousness of its opposite—because it is the only payment which he finds leisure to render. He must therefore represent it as so genuine and fervent, as to compensate the omission of other less easy services. But while he remains thus inactive, the only symptom by which the intensity of his belief can be appreciated, is the strength of his hostility towards the sceptic. Sentiments and acts of antipathy are thus the only proofs of allegiance which he can adduce, to place him on a level with the more scrupulous adherent. The hatred of the latter is of course ensured towards a disbelief, which would fain reduce his pious sacrifices to the level of ridiculous self-denial.

By all these conspiring motives the antipathy against atheists is engendered and provoked. Its diffusion too is most universal; for it is the single feeling in which the votaries of all systems of natural religion coincide, and direct their enmity to one common subject.

2. The antipathy against non-observance is inferior; both in extent and in vehemence, to that against unbelief. There is not the same array of feelings to stimulate it. First, the dissent is by no means so wide and radical as in the former case—indeed in many instances the difference of conduct may involve scarcely any variance of opinion at all, but is referable to the superior presence and urgency of human motives, which govern the actions of the believer, in defiance of his entire conviction that he is thereby forfeiting his chance of posthumous happiness. There is too, a greater hope of procuring conformity from the non-observant believer, than of planting the root of persuasion in the atheist. The former recognises the same sovereignty and is enlisted in the same ranks: It seems only requisite to sound the word of command more loudly and impressively in his ears, in order to enforce the course of action which such an acknowledgement appears to entail. And the active

religionist possesses ample means of thus disturbing and awakening a mind which suffers his fundamental principles to pass unquestioned. Whereas the atheist is deaf to these sonorous and impassioned appeals; and must be won by the cool and measured advances of reason. Secondly, the observant believer does not feel himself to be an object of contempt with the non-observant. The latter is even interested in admiring and eulogizing acts of devotion which he will not imitate, since by this encouragement to the worship of others, he lightens the criminality of his own neglect.

For these and other reasons, the antipathy which religion generates against non-observance, is far from being so virulent as that against unbelief. Indeed, unbelief necessarily implies entire non-observance, with scarcely any prospect of future amendment. While almost every believer is occasionally and to some extent obedient in practice, or at least recognizes the propriety of being so at a subsequent period.

Notwithstanding, however, this comparative deduction, there still remains a very strong enmity towards non-observance, whether in the way of neglect or of trespass. Ascetics, reposing their title to the esteem of mankind on a voluntary abnegation of particular enjoyments, naturally endeavour to fasten obloquy on all who indulge in them; Of course the ascetics hate him whom their interest leads them thus to injure. Besides, there exists in their minds, (though on most occasions perhaps unknown to themselves) a secret apprehension that their uncomplying neighbour may at last prove correct in his calculation, and that all their own self-denial may be thrown away. Yet it is a risk which they themselves do not choose to brave; and they, therefore, would fain deter any one else from undertaking it. Both vexation and envy thus impel them to enforce this prohibition in the most effectual manner—that is by forestalling the post-obituary sentence, and encompassing the path of self-indulgence with all the evils which earthly abuse and hostility can devise. Their own mistrust of the result is evinced by their reluctance to allow to the sinner the unmolested profit or loss of his own temerity.

3. The third species of antipathy which remains to be noticed, is that upon the score of mal-observance—a feeling more virulent than the second species, though less so than the first. In proportion to the stress we lay upon our mode of serving and obeying the Deity, will be the abhorrence with which we regard any rival system of worship. The ritual enjoined by the latter appears in our eyes a perversion of holy ordinances and institutions—frequently indeed we view it as the most flagrant impiety. We have ourselves always been taught to venerate a certain class of practices, as strictly agreeable to the Deity: But here is another nation who lay claim to his favour by very opposite performances, and mere natural religion unhappily furnishes us with no rational ground for preferring our own. Thus deficient in reasons, we naturally endeavour to deter people from demanding any, or even from whispering doubts which might call for a solution. Dogmatical assumption of our own tenets; the bitterest invective against all who question them; these are the expedients which have been universally employed for this purpose. The first secures to the doctrine the only support which circumstances admit, that is, our own authority, derived from the credit we have acquired in other cases for judgment and penetration: The second terrifies the hearer from manifesting any difficulty of assent, by which he might himself incur the suspicion of partiality towards the enemies of our worship.

It thus appears that to him who entertains a strong conviction, for which he has little or no arguments to offer, an intense antipathy not only clings as the natural concomitant of dissent, but is even necessary as a weapon to intimidate unsatisfied hearers, and to stifle an enquiry which it would be difficult to ward off in any other manner. Unprepared for parley, he quickly resorts to that heavy artillery on which alone his reliance can be placed. Besides, the want of solid proof generates, in this case also, the same mistrust and apprehension of error as we have remarked in the former—and hence an equal aversion and hostility towards all men, who by adopting a different course of worship, excite these doubts in his mind.

The Pagan, who has from his earliest youth regarded his own ritual as exclusively conformable to the divine will, is disposed to imagine that the Hindoo, or any other nation whose religious practices are widely different, must be a candidate for the favour of some unseen Being distinct from the one whom he himself recognises. Natural religion cannot demonstrate to him that there is no more than one God; and it would be presumptuous in him to assume it without proof. It is natural, therefore, that he should regard the foreign votary as the servant of a different God. But to see his own Deity not only neglected, but forsaken in behalf of another, is exasperating in the extreme; since it sets a limit to the influence of the former, and brings forward a rival sovereignty, from which a different distribution of favour and displeasure is to be expected. To attest, therefore, the rectitude of his own choice and the superior might of his own Deity, he musters under the divine banners all the temporal force which he himself can command, for the purpose of crushing the rival worshippers, and terminating the influence of the unseen Being on whom they rely.

Mal-observance, like unbelief, includes non-observance; For the votary of a different system of religion will of course altogether neglect the ceremonies which I consider as the peculiar privilege of mine. But besides this, he braves my opinions, and heaps all the terms of moral reprobation on those practices which have always appeared to me the holiest and most essential: And there is scarcely a prospect of persuading him to adopt a conduct agreeable to my views, since we entertain so few common principles. It is natural, therefore, that I should detest him far more warmly than a simply remiss and disobedient fellow-believer.

Such is the antipathy which religion sows in the human bosom—and such are the principal shapes and varieties which it assumes. It is unhappily but too notorious, how fruitful this factitious hostility has proved in every species of destructive and sanguinary result. If we merely contemplate the fierce and merciless persecutions whose enormity has obtruded them upon the view of the historian, the misery thus introduced will appear sufficiently atrocious and revolting. But it is not by these extreme barbarities that the largest aggregate of suffering is occasioned. Very shocking instances of cruelty must be comparatively rare, from the desperation and inextinguishable thirst of vengeance which they are sure to provoke; and they are rather to be viewed as indicating the pitch of fury to which the antipathy will occasionally stimulate mankind, than as aiding our measurement of its evil effects. These are to be estimated by computing the degree to which it is current and universal—the average force with which it acts at all times upon the bulk of the community. The very same principles, which at times breaks out into such ferocious excesses, is eternally at work, provoking innumerable manifestations of lesser hostility and ill-will—and these acts, although less injurious when individually considered, yet abundantly compensate this defect by their ceaseless recurrence and ubiquity.

It is not easy to estimate the total sum of evil introduced by this means—but when we contemplate the universal prevalence of religious hatred, and its daily and hourly interference with the line of human conduct—creating factitious motives for inflicting mutual evil, or witholding assistance—we shall be authorised in placing to its account no inconsiderable portion of the misery which pervades human society. The notorious and extensive influence of this antipathy is no where more forcibly marked than in the arguments concerning toleration. It is only within the last century, or a little before, that philosophy has ventured to broach the doctrine of toleration—that is, to recommend the propriety of tolerating, or *enduring*, the existence of persons entertaining different religious sentiments. Previous to this the understood principle, as well as practice, appears to have been, that no one could be expected to *endure* persons dissenting from him on religious subjects. Intolerance was then the universally acknowledged credential of sincerity, and, indeed, still remains so, wherever the preponderance of any one pious fraternity is so complete, as to render this non-endurance of dissenters at all practicable. It is chiefly the growing equilibrium between different sects which has engendered this mutual suspension of arms, and mitigated the fury of religious antipathy.

MISCHIEF II—PERVERTING THE POPULAR OPINION—CORRUPTING MORAL SENTIMENT—SANCTIFYING ANTIPATHY—PRODUCING AVERSION TO IMPROVEMENT.

To ensure on the part of every individual a preference of actions favourable to the happiness of the community, it is essentially requisite that that community should themselves be able to recognise what is conducive to their happiness—that they should manifest a judgment sufficiently precise and untainted to separate virtue from vice. The reason why the popular sanction is generally mentioned as an encouragement to good and a restraint upon bad conduct, is, because the major part of the society are supposed in most cases to know what benefits and what injures them—and that they are disposed to love and recompense the former behaviour, to hate and punish the latter. Now the efficacy of the public hate, considered as a restraint upon mis-deeds, depends upon its being constantly and exclusively allied with the real injury of the public—upon its being uniformly called forth whenever their happiness is endangered, and never upon any mistaken or imaginary alarms. Whatever, therefore, tends to make men hate that which does not actually hurt them, contributes to distort or disarm public opinion, in its capacity of a restraint upon injurious acts—for the public sentiment is only the love or hatred of all or most of the individuals in the society.

Now religion has been shewn to create a number of factitious antipathies—that is, to make men hate a number of practices which they would not have hated had their views been confined simply to the present life. But if men would not naturally have hated these practices, this is a proof that they are not actually hurtful. Religion, therefore, attaches the hatred of mankind to actions not really injurious to them, and thus seduces it from its only legitimate and valuable function, that of deterring individuals from injurious conduct.

By this distortion from its true purpose, the efficacy of the popular censure is also weakened on those occasions when it is most beneficially and indispensibly called for, as a guardian of human happiness. It is dissipated over an unnecessary extent of defensible ground, and thus becomes less efficient at every particular point; And it is deprived of that unity of design, and that reference to a distinct and assignable end, which marks all provisions exclusively destined for securing the public happiness. The different actions, to which the public odium is attached, appear entirely unconnected and heterogeneous in their tendencies, and its application is thus involved in darkness and confusion.

Besides, hatred from one man towards another, is a feeling decidedly noxious, and no friend of humanity could suffer a single drop of it to exist, were it not required to prevent a greater evil—to obviate a still larger destruction of happiness. Unless sanctified by this warrant, the affection of hatred becomes nothing better than unredeemed malignity. It is by exciting and keeping alive this malignity, that religion enforces her causeless prohibitions; and, therefore her influence is injurious, not only by obstructing an innocuous gratification, but by all the malice and animosity which she plants in the human bosom in order to effect her purpose. A pernicious restriction is thus completed by still more pernicious means.

Though this is the most mischievous species of corruption with which the popular opinion can be infected, it is not, however, the only one. Its encouragements, as well as its restraints, may be seduced and mis-applied. To promote its true aim, the public favour and esteem ought to be as inseparably and exclusively annexed to beneficial practices, as its hatred to acts of a contrary tendency. But religion never fails to conciliate a very material share of credit for practices, which, however meritorious with reference to a posthumous state, cannot be affirmed to produce any temporal advantage, and therefore would never have been esteemed had our views been confined to the present life. She thus draws off a portion of the popular favour, from its legitimate task of encouraging acts conducive to human felicity: She cheats the public into the offer of a reward for conduct always useless, sometimes injurious—and embezzles part of the fund consecrated to the national service, for bribery on the personal behalf of the monarch.

The popular sanction, thus mis-applied both in its encouraging and restrictive branches, may become the unconscious instrument of evil to almost any extent. It may criminate and inderdict any number of innocent enjoyments, like the eating of pork—or any acts however extensively useful, like loans of money upon interest. And it may heap profuse veneration on monastic stripes and self-denial, or ratify the cruelty which persecution inflicts upon the unhappy dissenter.

But the public never praise an action without thinking it to deserve praise, nor blame one without believing it to deserve blame. This mis-direction, therefore, of praise and blame naturally and necessarily introduces a false apprehension of what is praise-worthy and blame-worthy. The practices thus erroneously imagined to merit their esteem become enrolled in the catalogue of virtues—those falsely conceived to merit their censure are represented as vices. Thus the terms of moral approbation and blame are deceitfully transferred to actions which a regard to the public happiness would not legitimate, and the science of morality is cast into utter darkness and embarrassment, by the removal of that light which an unity of standard could alone have imparted.

This misapplication of terms is farther confirmed by the language used in addressing or characterising the Deity. We have already shewn that the Almighty, though always actually conceived by natural religion as a capricious despot, is yet never described except in epithets of the most superlative and unmingled praise. The practices, which he is supposed to approve or delight in, will of course be characterised in language the same as that which is applied to himself. What he loves, will be laudable or virtuous—what he dislikes, blameable or vicious. To sacrifice the life of a human being becomes thus entitled to the name of a good action, when enjoined (or supposed to be enjoined) by the Being whom every one calls all-beneficent and perfect. It matters not what the action is—so it be agreeable to the just and good Creator, it must itself be necessarily just and good.

By these two concurrent causes, the science of morality has been enveloped in a cloud of perplexity and confusion. Philosophers profess, by means of this science, to interpret and to reconcile the various applications of approving and disapproving terms. But the practices on which the same epithet of approbation is bestowed, appear so incurably opposite, that it has been found impossible to reduce them to one common principle, or to discover any constituent quality which universally attracts either praise or blame. The intellect has been completely bewildered and baffled in all attempts to explain the foundation of morality, or to find any unerring fingerpost amidst a variety of diverging paths.

Hence the same misdirection of eulogy and censure, by which mankind have been deluded into favouring those who did them harm, and persecuting their benefactors, has given birth besides to another unhappy effect. The science of morality has become so doubtful and embarrassed, so destitute of all centre and foundation, as to lose all authority, and to be incapable either of rectifying current mistakes, or guarding against future ones. By the depravation of this all important science, therefore, these misdirections not only secure themselves from all trial or scrutiny, but also ensure a similar success and immunity to any future prejudices. For the moralist, comparing the various actions to which praise or blame is awarded, and finding not the smallest analogy either in their nature or tendency, some being beneficial, others hurtful, others indifferent—is unable to range them under any common exponent, and accordingly sets them down in a catalogue one after another, as distinct and heterogeneous dictates of a certain blind and unaccountable impulse, which he terms a *moral instinct* or *conscience*. In cases where all men agree in approving or disapproving the same practice, he appeals to this universal consent as an invincible testimony to the justice of the feeling, and extols the uniformity of nature's voice: in cases where they differ, he compliments the particular sect or public, for whom he writes, as having singly adhered to the path of right and the dictates of nature, and bastardizes the rest of mankind as an outcast and misguided race.

The science of morality having been thus degraded into a mere catalogue of the reigning sentiments, without any trial or warrant, not only do the prejudices of to-day meet with adoption and licence, but a sanctuary is also provided for those of to-morrow. Morality cannot, in this state, either instruct or amend mankind, nor is it capable of progress or improvement, because the standard, by which alone its advance can be measured, has been cast away. To this stagnant and useless condition it has been reduced by the excessive misapplications of praise and blame, which religion has to so large an extent occasioned, though other causes have doubtless contributed to the same end.

We should not omit to remark, that as all means of distinguishing right from wrong disapprobation is obliterated, every one naturally endeavours to licence and sanctify his own private antipathies, by placing them to the account of religion. By an artful transfer of terms, he attempts to slip his personal dislike into the moral code, and to found thereon the character of being zealously concerned for the honour of God and the interests of virtue. If he can succeed in procuring a few allies, his antipathy becomes gradually diffused and legalised, and is worshipped as a dictate of the moral sense. But in order to obtain these partisans, he is compelled to offer some service in return; and for this purpose he naturally stands forth as the champion of their antipathies, in the same manner as they second his. By this compromise, therefore, the whole band are leagued to endorse and accredit each others enmities, and to vilify the actions which they dislike, as infringements of religion and of the law of nature. The less hurtfull the action—the less real necessity can be alleged for the dislike—the more loudly will they be obliged to appeal to religion and the moral instinct, as their only chance of shelter from the charge of absurd peculiarity. Those antipathies, therefore, which are the least defensible on the score of public utility, are the most commonly put forward to be stamped and sanctified by religion, and to pass current under the denomination of laws of nature.

One consequence and manifestation of this principle is so

important as to deserve particular notice. An aversion towards improvement is its decided effect—and where such a feeling previously existed, it is both aggravated in force, and hardened against all question and scrutiny.

The sequences and concatenation of phenomena, as presented to our senses, and subsequently compared and classified, form what is called *the course of nature*, supposed to be established by the Deity. All fresh facts, all acquisition and application of knowledge, introduce a change in these sequences, and therefore break in upon the laws of nature.

Now the laws of nature, conceived as they are to be the arrangements of the Deity, acquire a character of supreme holiness, and to infringe them is supposed to be an impious defeat and counteraction of the divine will. The same being, indeed, who originally set them on foot, may suspend or over-rule them, if he will; But any interference for this purpose, on the part of man, is presumptuous and unwarrantable in the highest degree. To counteract the course of nature, and to oppose a bar to the designs of the Deity, are in fact synonymous phrases, and therefore all alterations in the course of nature are so many obstacles, daringly presented by feeble man against the designs of his creator.

Agreeable to this, the epithet *unnatural* indicates perhaps the most severe, aggravated, and relentless odium ever harboured in the human bosom. It is perfectly self-justifying, nor does the accused dare to call for any proof or testimony in support of the change: it is also quite irresistible, and no plea can be heard in mitigation of its effect.

Now all successive discoveries and their application to fact, constitute so many alterations of the laws of nature. But no discovery is ever applied except for the purpose of augmenting human comfort—for there is no other motive to employ it. Consequently all augmentation of human happiness, by an improved knowledge of facts, is *unnatural*, or contrary to the laws of nature: that is, it is an impious counteraction of the designs of God. It naturally therefore becomes the object of the bitterest religious antipathy, and all practical improvement is thus pre-extinguished and stifled in the birth, by the sweeping epithet of *unnatural.*

It is vain to urge, that the fact falsifies these conclusions—that the promotion of human comfort, by means of an augmented knowledge of the passing phenomena, is never proscribed and regarded as opposite to the divine will, except in a few particular cases; while in the greater number of instances no one ever introduces the supposition. It is sufficient for my purpose to shew that this effect is produced in a certain number of cases; more in some climates and ages, fewer in others—that practices conducive to human happiness have been branded and repelled simply on the ground of being unnatural. For this is satisfactory evidence that natural religion has a tendency to engender an hostility to improvement; and that if the tendency does not manifest and realize itself, in every particular instance, this is because other causes operate in counteraction of it.

The increase of light and wisdom throughout Europe, has, indeed happily tended to dispel this error, and to restrict the application of such an interdict against improvement to a comparatively small number of cases, wherein either peculiar prejudices, or injury to some powerful sinister interest, act with more than usual effect upon the antipathies of mankind. But still the interdict exists; and it is only the dissentient voice of public opinion which suspends its execution. For whenever sentence is passed against any particular mode of amelioration, it is always by virtue of the standing enactment against all—that is by accusations of contrariety to the laws of nature and the designs of the Deity; which would, if pursued consistently, prohibit all improvement whatever. And the only scheme for parrying such an accusation is borrowed from this inconsistency, and general non-execution of the enactment: "You do not object to an alteration of the laws of nature for purposes of human happiness, in such and such cases—Why awaken your sleeping restriction here, and attach so much criminality to this particular plan, simply on the score of being unnatural or an innovation upon the laws of Nature?"

There has been a period when religion was arrayed to silence the discoveries of Galileo, and to prohibit physical and medicinal improvements, such as the emetic. If such sentences are no longer hazarded now, it is not from any change in the spirit and tendency of the law, but from its progressive weakness and loss of dominion, the natural result of the diffusion of knowledge.

MISCHIEF III—DISQUALIFYING THE INTELLECTUAL FACULTIES FOR PURPOSES USEFUL IN THIS LIFE.

There are several modes in which religion tends to unfit the mental faculties for the promotion of the mere temporal happiness of mankind. Considered with reference to a posthumous existence, indeed, which divines justly regard as far more important than the present, her influence may be highly beneficial in qualifying us for the lot there to be awarded. But these magnificent promises cannot be realized without a transient loss in this preparatory state—and amongst all the modes in which this loss is incurred, few are more serious than the disqualification of our intellects.

SECTION I—*DISJOINING BELIEF FROM EXPERIENCE.*

It has been remarked in the early part of this volume, that the primary and unsolicited provision of nature consists for the most part of pains and wants—that the means of soothing the one and satisfying the other, were the gradual and toilsome discovery of man, even now far from being perfected—that consequently all pleasure, and exemption from suffering, was the fruit of knowledge. If a man does not know the way to avoid or to remedy an impending pain, he will be compelled to suffer it: If he does not know the way to procure any particular pleasure, the pleasure will not seek him of its own accord, and he will, therefore, be obliged to forego it.

But all our knowledge with regard to pleasure and pain is derived from experience. To know the way of procuring the former and escaping the latter, some one must have made trial. Knowledge can only be instrumental for these purposes, when it is the statement and summary of the trials which have thus been made.

Now knowledge consists in the belief of certain facts: All useful knowledge, therefore, (that is, all which can be instrumental in multiplying the enjoyments and diminishing the sufferings of this life) consists in believing facts conformable to experience—in believing the modes of producing pleasure and avoiding pain to be, in each particular case, such as actual trial indicates. It is on the conformity of belief with experience, therefore, that the attainment of pleasure and the prevention of misery, in every case without exception, is founded.

Such is the inestimable value, indeed, the essential and overwhelming necessity, of belief conformable to experience. Belief unconformable to experience is not applicable, in any degree, to the removal of unhappiness, or the production of enjoyment; and consequently is altogether useless. The whole utility of belief, therefore, consists in this conformity.

To maintain and extend the alliance between belief and experience will thus appear to be incalculably the most important object of human endeavour. Whatever promotes such an attempt, must be considered as a most valuable instrument for the augmentation of happiness; since this is the only means by which it can be augmented. And conversely, whatever tends to disjoin belief from experience, must be regarded as crippling, to a greater or less extent, the sole engine by which our preservation even from incessant suffering is ensured, and tending to disqualify our mental faculties for purposes of temporal happiness.

Such is the injurious effect (with reference to the present life) of disjoining the two—or of making us believe any thing uncertified by experience. Who ever acts upon such an uncertified persuasion, or induces any one else to act upon it, can never attain any benefit by it, and may occasion very serious evil. Indeed all human errors are only so many manifestations of this unsanctioned belief.

As all real facts, or instances of belief thus certified, mutually hang together and tend to support each other, so that he who acquires any one is thereby assisted and placed in a better condition for the acquisition of more—in the same manner all errors, or uncertified persuasions, though heterogeneous and discordant one with another, yet conspire all to one common end, that of deranging the conformity of belief to experience. Each separate instance of this want of conformity engenders others, and renders the mind less likely to keep close to a conformable belief upon other occasions. Every particular instance, therefore, besides the mis-calculations to which it may directly and of itself give birth, is injurious by the general habit of derangement which it creates in the mental system—by preparing the intellect to be at other periods the recipient of useless or uncertified belief. You cannot impress upon the mind one such persuasion, without rendering it liable to the incursions of others to any extent.

He, for example, who reposes faith in the accounts of Lilliput and Brobdignag, must have a mind so constituted, as to believe on many other occasions without the warrant of experience. We should mark our sense of this by attaching less credit to his opinions, and describing him under appropriate epithets of inferiority. We should readily admit that such a peculiarity of mind comparatively incapacitated him from directing either his own conduct or ours to any salutary purpose. If this disposition to uncertified belief spreads still farther in his mind, and manifests itself in a considerable number of cases, we then term it insanity. His belief then becomes not only useless for our guidance, but imminently dangerous and threatening to our security. Accordingly we do not permit it to direct even his own actions, but immediately subject his body to a foreign super-intendance.

Such are the unhappy consequences produced by a deviation of belief from experience. This disjunction, when frequent and embracing subjects of importance, constitutes insanity, and renders an individual utterly incapable of providing for his own happiness, as well as a destructive foe to that of his fellow-creatures: When rare and confined to trifling subjects, it causes a proportionably slighter depravation of his mental faculties, but never fails to impair in a greater or less degree, his competency of judging for the welfare of himself and of others. It is most important to keep in mind, that madness with all its dreadful consequences is only a total divorce of belief from experience—that all intellectual weakness is the fruit of this divorce to a lesser extent—and that every separate instance in which such a disjunction is effected, by whatever cause it may be, lays the mind open to the attacks of other disjoining causes; thus creating a disease which is sure to spread.

Having thus exposed the enormous evils which result from the disjunction of belief from experience, I proceed to show the modes in which natural religion inevitably causes such a disjunction.

1. The fundamental tenet of natural religion is, the persuasion that there exists a Being unseen, unheard, untouched, untasted, and unsmelt—his place of residence unknown—his shape and dimensions unknown—his original beginning undiscovered. This is what the negative terms *invisible, omnipresent, infinite*, and *eternal*, imply.

Now the very description of this Being obviously shews, that no one can ever have had any experience of his existence. To have experience of any thing external to ourselves, supposes certain concomitant circumstances—the exercise of one of our senses—a definite time and place of existence—a particular size and figure. Without these concomitants, experience cannot take place, and the sublime conception of infinite attributes at once negatives them all. You cannot state that God is in a particular place, because that would imply that he was not in any other place—since the only intent of particularization is to exclude every thing except that which is specified. Our persuasion, therefore, of God cannot be founded upon experience.

The very basis, therefore, of natural religion is an article of *extra-experimental belief*, or of belief altogether unconformable to experience. It has a tendency, thus in the very outset, to introduce that mental depravation which we have demonstrated to be the inevitable result of this species of belief. I do not here intend to assert that the doctrine in question is untrue, but merely to point out the peculiarity of the evidence on which it rests—that it is a persuasion uncertified by experience, and, therefore, vitiating the intellect so far as regards mere temporal interests. Whether true or untrue, in either case, the very nature of the belief occasions it to produce the same disqualifying effect upon the mental faculties.

2. Our belief with regard to the original creative power of

God, and the design with which it was exerted, is alike uncertified by experience. No man has ever had experience of the commencement of things: And, therefore, whatever account we admit as to their origin, our belief must be *extra-experimental.* If the interests of the present life require that our persuasion should never deviate from experience, they also require that we should not attempt to account for the original commencement of things—because it is obvious that experience must be entirely silent upon that subject.

The belief in design, as dictating the exertion of this creative power, is alike *extra-experimental.* Experience exhibits to us design only in man and animals; and in them its effects are confined to the displacement of matter, and the admotion or amotion of its particles to and from each other. This is all which experience shews us to be produced by design; and we cannot believe that it produces any other effects, without falling into the disease of *extra-experimental* persuasion.

Besides, to say that the human body, or the universe, was brought into the order which we now see, by design—this supposes a previous state in which the parts of the human body were lying about in a heap—fibres in one place, brain in another, membranes and muscles in a third—without the least tendency to combine together and form a whole. Design pre-supposes the existence of substances endued with certain properties, and can only be pretended to account for their transition, from one relative situation called *confusion*, to another called *order*. But has any one ever had experience of this preliminary chaos?

Again, an omnipotent will is something which is by its very nature placed beyond the reach of experience. Were we permitted indeed to introduce the supposition of omnipotence, this would materially facilitate the explanation of all other difficult points, as well as that of the original of things. Any thing will solve the difficulty, provided you are allowed to render it omnipotent. Instead of supposing a *will* which can perform every thing, you may suppose *fire* or *water* which can perform every thing, and all results are equally well explained. Why was Epicurus forced into such absurdities in attempting to explain all phenomena by the doctrine of atoms, or Thales by that of water? From the difficulty of reconciling these phenomena with atoms or water of limited power and properties. Had they dared to discard openly these limitations, the difficulty of the task would have vanished. When the fairy with her all-powerful wand has once been introduced, it is as easy to explain the sudden rise of a palace as of a cottage.

These considerations, we think, clearly demonstrate that all belief in design, as having been originally instrumental in forming the world, is completely *extra-experimental.*

3. Nor less so is the belief that the Deity will in a posthumous existence distribute to us certain pleasures and pains. It is plain that whatever be the evidence on which this persuasion is built, experience teaches us nothing about it.

4. Another case of *extra-experimental* conviction implanted by religion is, the belief of God's agency in the present life. As it is in this case that the mischiefs flowing from such uncertified belief assume the most determinate and palpable shape, we shall examine it at greater length than the rest.

You believe that the Deity interferes occasionally to modify the train of events in the present life. Your belief is avowedly unconformable to experience, for the very essence of the divine interposition is to be extrinsic and irreconcileable to the course of nature. But mark the farther consequances: You dethrone and cancel the authority of experience in every instance whatever; and you thus place yourself out of condition to prove any one fact, or to disprove any other.

What steps do you take to prove that a man has committed

murder? You produce a witness who saw him level his pistol at the head of the deceased, heard the report, and beheld the man drop. But this testimony drives all its persuasive force from the warrant and countersign of experience. Without this it is perfectly useless. Unless I know by previous experience that eye witnesses most commonly speak the truth—that a pistol ball takes the direction in which it is levelled and not the opposite—I should never be convinced, by the attestation of these particular facts, of that ulterior circumstance which you wish me to infer. To complete the proof, two things are requisite; the previous lessons of experience, and the applicability of these lessons to the present case. But no such application can take place unless the course of nature remains the same as it was before. A gratuitous assumption must therefore be made, that the course of nature continues inviolate and uniform. But to assume this in every particular case, is to assume the universal inviolability of the laws of nature.

Whoever therefore believes these laws to be violable at the will of an incomprehensible Being, completely debars himself from the application of all previous experience to the existing fact. If they are violable at all, why may they not have been violated in the case before us? No imaginable reason can be assigned for this—because in order to constitute a reason—in order to make a complete proof—you must presuppose that uniformity of the course of nature which your reason is intended to vindicate. Whether you assume her laws to be violable or inviolable, you must adhere to the same assumption throughout. If you say that they are inviolable, you cannot maintain them to be infringed in any particular case—if you hold that they are violable, you cannot assume them to be permanent and uniform in any one case.

If therefore you believe the agency of an incomprehensible Being in the affairs of this life, your belief is such as would, were it pursued consistently, exclude you from all application of past experience to the future—and therefore incapacitate you from contriving any defence against coming pains, or any modes of procuring pleasures.

Again, this belief also precludes you from applying the process of refutation, and thus from detecting any falsehood whatever. For no assertion can ever be refuted except by offering proof of some other assertion, and then appealing to experience for a certificate of the incompatibility of the two. A man clears himself from an alleged crime by proving an alibi. The whole virtue of this defence rests upon the presumption, that experience attests the impossibility of performing a certain act at more than a certain distance. If it is suggested that the laws of nature are violable—if it is questioned whether the previous lessons of experience are applicable to this particular case—then, inasmuch as no evidence of their applicability can be adduced, the process of disproof is at once nullified. The inviolability of the course of nature must be gratuitously assumed as the root from which all incompatibility between any two assertions, and therefore all proof of the falsehood of either, is derived.

Hence the belief of an unseen agent, infringing at pleasure the laws of nature, appears to be pregnant with the most destructive consequences. It discredits and renders inadmissible the lessons of experience: It vitiates irrecoverably the processes both of proof and refutation, thereby making truth incapable of being established, and falsehood incapable of being detected: It withdraws from us the power of distinguishing the true methods, of procuring enjoyment or avoiding pain, from the fase ones; and plunges us into the naked, inexperienced and helpless condition of a newborn child—thereby qualifying us indeed for the kingdom of heaven, but leaving us wholly defenceless against the wants and sufferings of earth.

I do not indeed affirm that this *extra-experimental* belief has actually produced—what if adhered to with consistency, it ought to produce—an entire mistrust of all experience. The necessity for a general reliance on the stability of nature has been too powerful to be resisted—and therefore mankind have shuffled off the dangerous consequences by their usual resort of inconsistency—sometimes assuming the lessons of experience as supreme and incontestable, sometimes disregarding them as arbitrary and variable at the will of an incomprehensible Being. But though this *extra-experimental* belief has been thus only partially entertained and confined to a corner of the mind, its pernicious effects have still been very great—and I shall proceed to specify an instance of the manner in which it tends to disable the intellect, and to expunge all the criteria of truth and falsehood.

It is not many years since witchcraft was recognized and prohibited as an actual offence, and persons tried and condemned for committing it. To attempt a defence against such an accusation was obviously impracticable. The essence of the crime consisted in an alliance with demons, who could at pleasure interrupt the course of nature; and therefore it availed nothing though the defendant could prove an unexceptional alibi. He might, by the assistance of his hyperphysical ally, have ridden an hundred miles through the air in as many seconds. Nor was it possible to determine what facts were or were not inconsistent with commission of the crime; or consequently, to adduce any thing like exculpatory testimony. The defendant was thus laid completely at the mercy of the favour or aversion of judges unguided by any rational inference, as may be seen by consulting any of the old trials for this imaginary offence.

All the unhappy victims who have been condemned for witchcraft may be considered as one instance of the wretched effects of *extra-experimental* belief; as sacrifices occasioned by that thorough depravation of the intellect, and erasure of the distinction between truth and falsehood, which it is the nature of this belief to effect whenever it reigns within the mind. The number of men thus condemned publicly has been far from inconsiderable—not to mention those who have undergone private persecution and suspicion from their neighbourhood; a body probably more numerous, though less exposed to notice.

As this persuasion utterly disqualifies mankind for the task of filtering truth from falsehood, so the multitude of fictitious tales for which it has obtained credence and currency in the world, exceeds all computation. To him who believes in the intervention of incomprehensible and unlimited Beings, no story can appear incredible. The most astonishing narratives are exempted from cross-examination, and readily digested under the title of miracles or prodigies. Of these miracles, every nation on the face of the earth has on record and believes thousands. And as each nation disbelieves all except its own, each, though it believes a great many, yet disbelieves more. The most enthusiastic believer in miracles, therefore, cannot deny that an enormous excess of false ones have obtained credence amongst the larger portion of mankind. The root of all these fictions, by which the human intellect has thus been cheated and overrun, is the *extra-experimental* belief of the earthly interference of God; and the immense evil arising from such a deception is another of its pernicious results.

Nor should we omit, in reckoning up these results, the universal prevalence of the expectations arising out of this belief in particular interpositions of the Deity. Entertaining this conviction, a man is of course led to frame some conjecture on what occasions the unseen Being will be likely to interpose. He naturally selects those, on which his anticipations are most at fault, and when he is most ignorant what real event is to be expected. In this state the experimental belief ceases to suggest any predictions, and the *extra-experimental* of course steps into the vacant chair and assumes the rod of prophecy. Hence, instead of adopting the most skilful expedients which a comparison of the known phenomena would suggest, his behaviour will be determined either by some accidental and incomprehensible peculiarity of circumstance, or by certain deceitful and irrelevant conceptions of the divine attributes.

It would be both useless and impracticable to enumerate all those trifling casualties which have, in one place or another, been regarded as manifestations of God's interference. The flight of birds—the neighing of a horse—the drawing of lots—and a thousand other such inconsequential incidents have been consulted as instructors and guides to human short-sightedness, and as interpreters of the divine decrees. To disregard one of them was considered as an act of impiety, and contempt of a special warning. The phenomena thus selected have been infinitely various—the doctrine and principle exactly similar throughout.

To illustrate the depravation of judgment produced by these expectations of divine interference, it is important to remark their effect when recognized and acted upon in the system of judicature—a province wherein, as it demands the most complete preparation and use of the faculties, all mistaken principles are the most prominently displayed.

The trial by ordeal has been most universally approved and established, in the infancy at least of all societies, from Hindostan to America. Unable to discover satisfactory criteria of guilt and innocence, by a just comparison of conflicting testimony, mankind have endeavoured to extricate themselves from the uneasy feelings of doubt, by a blind reliance on the *extra-experimental* belief. In confidence that the point would be decided for them, they have abandoned the task of determining it for themselves, and have been contented with executing what they regarded as the divine verdict. Now certainly if the Deity is ever in any case believed to interpose, this is the occasion of all others when his interposition would be most naturally and most rationally anticipated, supposing him truly benevolent. Were a chief-justice animated by genuine benevolence, his feelings would not permit him to remain inactive, when his efforts might extricate the innocent from impending punishment, or expose the shifts of the guilty.

But though this is by far the most defensible case in which divine interpositions have ever been looked for, we hear it unanimously treated, by writers of present day, as a symptom of the most pitiable imbecility—as utterly incompetent to elicit the truth—and as the most cruel distortion of penal judicature. The miserable effects which a belief in the temporal agency of God has produced, in this case alone without mentioning others, are incalculable. Reflect on the number of persons whom the issue of the ordeal has consigned to unmerited torture, or protected from an appropriate penalty—on the bar thus opposed to all improvement in the judicial process—on the extension of this method of lottery to all other matters of doubt, which its reception in the sacred field of judicature would countenance: Consider too that these evils still infest perhaps the larger portion of the globe, and all the uninstructed nations who inhabit it. This immense mass of misfortune flows from one particular application—and that too the most rationally deduced from the current hypothesis—of the belief in the temporal interference of the Deity.

The example which has been just cited is of great value, because we there behold the belief in superhuman agency applied to a distinct and particular case, and thence producing consequences which it is impossible to shuffle over or evade. These consequences are universally admitted to be most pernicious, in the instance of ordeal—and similar effects cannot fail to result, whenever the same belief is elsewhere entertained and applied to action. He who feel confidence that the Deity will decide for him a particular point, or realise any other object of his wishes, will of course take no pains to form his own opinion, or to attain the object by his own efforts. Reliance on foreign aid, if perfect and full, supersedes the necessity of self-exertion altogether—and if the person thus relying puts himself to any trouble whatever, it is only because his confidence is not perfect. A man sits still while his servant is bringing up breakfast, because he feels quite confident that his desires will be attained without any trouble of his own. The belief therefore in superhuman interference cannot fail, when firmly and thoroughly entertained, to produce an entire abandonment of the means suggested by experience for human enjoyment. If the Almighty declares against us, our efforts are fruitless—if in our favour, they are unnecessary: In neither case therefore have we any motive to make efforts.

Expectation of effects on the ground of the divine attributes must thus, so far as it is really genuine and operative, extinguish all forecast, and cut all the sinews of human exertion. It must produce this effect whenever it produces any at all; and if such a result is not actually brought about, it is only because the nullity of the expectation has been in part exposed, and its influence proportionally weakened.

Any doctrine may be stated as having a tendency to introduce those consequences which are consistently and legitimately deducible from it—and while the doctrine is maintained in any one instance, there is always a chance that it will be extended to every other. He who looks for superhuman aid in one instance, is at least liable to do so on another. On this ground it is important to notice the mischievous tendency of these expectations, in a case where it would not be easy to trace home to them any palpable and specific evil consequences, such as those of the ordeal.

Expectations from the divine attribute of *pliability* have been and still continue universal. At least this is the foundation of the frequent prayers which are put up to Heaven for different species of relief—built, not upon the benevolence of God, for then his assistance would be extended alike to all the needy, whether silent or clamorous; but upon his yielding and accessible temper, which though indifferent if not addressed, becomes the warm and compliant partizan of every petitioner.

Now these expectations, supposing them well-founded and firmly entertained, cannot fail to introduce complete inactivity among the human race. Why should a man employ the slow and toilsome methods to which experience chains him down, when the pleasure which he seeks may be purchased by a simple act of prayer? Why should he plough, and sow, and walk his annual round of anxiety, when by the mere expression of a request, an omnipotent ally may be induced to place the mature produce instantly within his grasp? No, it is replied—God will not assist him unless he employs all his own exertions: he will not favour the lazy. In this defence however it is implied, either that the individual is not to rely upon God at all, in which case there is no motive to offer up the prayer—or that he is to feel a reliance, and yet act as if he felt none whatever. It is implied, therefore, that the conduct of the individual is to be exactly the same as if he did not anticipate any superhuman interference. By this defence, you do indeed exculpate the belief in supernatural agency from the charge of producing pernicious effects—because you reduce it to a mere non-entity, and make it produce no effects at all.

If therefore the request is offered up with any hope of being realised, it infallibly proves pernicious, by relaxing the efforts of the petitioner to provide for himself. Should he believe that God will, when he himself has done his utmost, make up the deficiency and crown his views with success; the effect will be to make him undertake any enterprizes whatever, without regarding the inadequacy of his means. Provided he employs actively all the resources in his power, he becomes entitled to have the balance made up from the divine treasury. "God never sends a child" (says the proverb) "but he sends food for it to eat." What is the natural inference from this doctrine, except that a man may securely marry without any earthly means of providing for his family, inasmuch as God will be sure to send him some?

What preserves the evil effects of this right of petitioning, which man is asserted to possess over the Deity, from the notoriety and exposure to which the consequences of the ordeal have been subjected—is, the very obscure and indistinct class of human wishes to which its exercise has gradually been restricted. Earthly discoveries and preparations are more commonly preferred for the satisfaction of our usual wants; nor are men so well contented with the provision which their heavenly Father has made for them, as to resign entirely all thought for the morrow. Some persons pray for their daily bread, it is true, and some do not; but every one without exception either works for it himself, or secures the services of some of his fellow-men. He who would wish to acquire a fortune or to learn a language, and contented himself with praying that God would transfer stock to him, or pour down the gift of tongues, would be derided as insane. If you ask a man whether he would rely upon petitions to Heaven for the accomplishment of any definite earthly wish, the incongruity of the means to the end appears then so glaring, that he thinks you are ridiculing him, although the language employed may be the gravest and most decorous. He will pray either for objects which he is sure to obtain with or without prayer, such as his daily bread—or for objects which he cannot tell whether he obtains or not, such as that the kingdom of God may come, that his will may be done in earth as it is heaven, etc. or for vague and indeterminate gifts, the fulfilment of which is not to be referred to any distinct time, such as health, longevity, good desires, etc. It is only by its results being thus, kept in the dark, that the inefficiency of prayer is protected from exposure.

I have thus analysed the several species of extra-experimental belief which religion begets in the mind, consisting in the persuasion of the existence, creative function, and agency both here and in a future life, of a supernatural Being. I have endeavoured to demonstrate from the very nature of this belief, that it cannot fail to disqualify the intellect for the pursuit of temporal happiness, more or less in proportion to the extent in which it is entertained. For as all our pleasure and all our exemption from want and pain, is the result of human provision—as these provisions are only so many applications of acquired knowledge, that is, of belief conformable to experience—it follows, that the whole fabric of human happiness depends upon the intimate and inviolable union between belief and experience. Whatever has the effect of disjoining the two, is decidedly of a nature to undermine and explode all the apparatus essential to human enjoyment—and if this result is not actually produced, it is only because the train laid is not sufficiently extensive, and is confined to the out-works instead of reaching the heart of the fortress. So far as any result at all is brought about, it is an advance towards the accomplishment of this work of destruction. And as every separate case, in which extra-experimental belief finds reception in the mind, paves the way for others, any one disjunction of belief from experience has a tendency to produce their entire and universal discordance.

MISCHIEF IV—SUBORNING UNWARRANTED BELIEF.

Akin to the foregoing mischief, though not precisely identical, is the distorting influence which religion exercises, by numbering belief in the catalogue of duties and merits—disbelief in that of crimes and offences. It has been already explained how, in the divine classification of human actions, disbelief is characterised as the most heinous of all trespasses, and belief as very meritorious, though not to a corresponding extent. The severest penalties are supposed and proclaimed to await the former; very considerable rewards to follow the latter.

So far as these threats and premiums are operative at all, the effect must be, to make a man believe that which he would not naturally have believed, and disbelieve that which he would not naturally have disbelieved. But in the natural state of things, a man assents to that which he thinks is supported by the best evidence—dissents from what appears to be refuted by the best evidence. Under such circumstances, there is nothing to guide his choice except the evidence. By holding out rewards to the former, and punishments to the latter, you introduce a lateral and extraneous force, which either wholly shuts out, or partially disturbs, the influence of the respective proofs. So far, therefore, as the reward is at all effective, it entices him to believe upon inadequate proof—so far as the punishment acts, it deters him from disbelieving upon adequate disproof.

Consult the analogy of common life. Is not the offer of a bribe to the judge universally reprobated, as disposing him to wrong and unauthorised decision? Is not a threatening letter to jurors recognised as tending to the same end? You might indeed allege, that the judge was honest, and the jurors intrepid; and, therefore, that bribe and threat were both ineffectual. But it would be impossible to controvert the pernicious tendency of these methods, supposing them to have any influence at all upon the verdict.

The religious premium offered for faith, tends in like manner to corrupt the judgment of an individual, and to foist in, by means of his hopes and partiality, a belief which unbiassed reason would not have tolerated. The penalties denounced against unbelief cooperate most powerfully, by enlisting his fears in behalf of the same self-deceit or hypocrisy.

There are, indeed, limits to the influence of rewards and punishments in thus engendering factitious belief. No man can, while this book is in his hand, make himself believe that it is not there. But though he cannot thus drive off sensation at pleasure; yet in matters where the truth does not obtrude itself so immediately, but must be gathered from various and wide-spread fragments of evidence, he can withdraw his thoughts from some, and fasten them upon others, almost to an unlimited extent. Hope and fear, constitute a motive for this undue preference; and his mind gravitates almost unconsciously towards the gainful side, as it shrinks from the terrors of the opposite prospect. He dwells on the positive proof of the promising doctrine, and sends his invention out in quest of additional reasons: while the negative is never permitted to occupy his attention for an instant. No wonder that the former, by thus exclusively absorbing the mind, assume a disproportionate value and magnitude, and appear irresistible, merely because nothing of an opposite tendency is allowed to join issue with them.

Such are the unjust and distorted movements of the intellect, which an interest in the result generally produces; and which the rewards and punishments respectively attached to belief or disbelief, must of course contribute to produce also.

This sort of reward, indeed, operates as a direct bounty upon credulity—that is, upon belief unsupported by sufficient and self-convincing evidence. The weaker the evidence, the greater is the merit in believing. This follows irresistibly. For if it is necessary to encourage belief by an artificial bounty, it would be useless to apply this stimulus to any doctrine which would of itself command the assent of mankind. The bounty must go where it is most needed; that is, to the support of doctrines which have little or no support of their own—and the largest slice of it to those which require the greatest encouragement, and would stand the least chance of being credited without it. Hence the less reason there is for receiving the doctrine, the larger share of merit will be awarded to the believer; and the tendency of the religious premium is thus to give birth to the most sweeping and indiscriminate credulity.

When assent or dissent has thus become a question of profit and loss, and not of reason, the believer is interested in bringing into contempt the guide whom he has deserted. He accordingly speaks in the most degrading terms of the fallibility and weakness of human reason, and of her incapacity to grasp any very lofty or comprehensive subject. It thus becomes a positive merit to decide contrary to reason, rather than with her.

But, with regard to provision of pleasure, and escape of pain in the present life, reason is admitted to be our only safe director. Whatever, therefore, throws discredit upon her, or makes mankind neglect or mistrust her decisions, places the mind in a state less likely to discern and follow the true path of human happiness. The rewards and punishments, which religion affixes respectively to belief and unbelief, have the most direct tendency to this state of blindness and confusion. They cannot fail to engender a habit of credulity; as well as a reluctance to examine, and an inability to poise, conflicting testimony. Of all mental qualities, this credulity is the weakest and most fatal, rendering a man an easy prey to deceit and error, and thereby exposing him to incessant disappointment and loss.

Suppose government were to offer large rewards to all who believed in witches, or in the personality and marvellous feats of Hercules or Jack the Giant-killer—and to threaten proportionate punishments to all disbelievers. No one would question that these offers and threats, if they were at all effective, would contribute to produce a general perversion of intellect—and that they would mislead men's judgments in numerous other cases besides that one to which they immediately applied. Error, when once implanted, uniformly and inevitably propagates its species.

Precisely the same in all cases, is the effect of erecting belief into an act of merit, and rendering unbelief punishable. You either produce no result at all; or you bribe and suborn a man into believing what he would not otherwise have believed—that is, what appears to him inadequately authenticated.

MISCHIEF V—DEPRAVING THE TEMPER.

That natural religion depraves the temper, and renders it infinitely less efficacious to the production of general happiness, has been shewn in the preceding Sections; inasmuch as it has been proved to engender virulent antipathies among mankind, or direct inclinations to harm each other. I propose to exhibit under the present head a farther deterioration of temper, referable to the same source; which does not announce itself in such palpable and violent injuries as the direct antipathy occasions, though its effects in corrupting the intercourse of life are most real and serious.

It may be asserted as a broad and general truth, that whatever curtails the personal comfort and happiness of any individual, disqualifies him to an equal extent from imparting happiness to his fellow-creatures; and not only thus much, but even disposes him to reduce, if possible, their quota of enjoyment to a level with his own. All the privations and misery, therefore, which religion inflicts upon an individual, extend through him to all those with whom he is placed in contact, and form a deduction from their happiness no less real and positive. Every particular species of private mischief enumerated in the preceding Chapter, is the parent of a train of misfortunes among the small fraternity which he is connected, by the unsocial and malevolent tone of mind which it inevitably generates in him.

There is also another mode in which religion still more effectually depraves the temper. The fitful and intermittent character of its inducements, incapable of keeping a steady purchase upon the mind, and daily overborne by urgent physical wants—the endless and most impracticable compliances exacted in its code—the misty attributes of its legislator, who treats every attempt to inquire into his proceedings as the most unpardonable of insults—all these render it quite impossible for a religionist to preserve any thing like a satisfactory accordance between his belief and his practice. Hence a perpetual uneasiness and dissatisfaction with himself—a sense of infirmity of purpose and dereliction of principle—which is thoroughly fatal to all calmness or complacency of mind. Privations or torture might by habit become tolerable and even indifferent: but this feeling of inferiority and degradation is continually renovated, and never ceases to vex the resolving and re-resolving sinner. And a mind thus at variance with itself can never be at peace with any body else, or feel sufficient leisure to sympathize with the emotions of others. It shelters its own vacillation under the plea of the general debasement and original wickedness of the whole human race: and this plea must assuredly weaken, if it does not entirely root out, all sympathy for such degenerate Beings.

Dissatisfied with his own conduct, it is hardly possible that a man can be satisfied with that of others. We are told indeed that this consciousness of imperfection in ourselves ought to engender humility, and indulgence towards the defects of our brethren. But rarely indeed does it produce any such effect as this. Its general tendency is to sharpen the edge of envy—to make us more acute in hunting out and magnifying the faults of others, inasmuch as nearly the sole comfort remaining to us is, the view of others equally distant from the same goal.

When we consider how infinitely the happiness of every family and society depends upon the steadiness and equability of disposition in each member, whereby all the rest are enabled to ascertain and avoid whatever might offend him—and upon the sympathy which each man manifests for the feelings of the remainder—the mischief above explained must be estimated very high in amount. There can be no equability of temper, where there is an unceasing conflict of principle and practice—of resolution and failure: and where the mind is darkened over by a sense of self-abasement and guilt. There can be no sympathy either for the enjoyments or the sufferings of others, where the thoughts of an individual are absorbed in averting posthumous torments or in entitling himself to a posthumous happiness—and where this object, important as it is, is involved in such obscurity, as to leave him in a state of perpetual anxiety and apprehension.

It is useless to affirm, that Religion does not in fact produce this unhappy result. If it does not, this is only because its motives cannot from their distance and uncertainty be made to act steadily and consistently upon the mind. So far as they do act, they tend to this result—and under peculiar circumstances, where the influence of the human motives is weakened or nearly removed, go far to accomplish it completely. Such is the case in monasteries, as may be seen by consulting the account of Don Leucadio Doblado, cited above.

MISCHIEF VI—CREATING A PARTICULAR CLASS OF PERSONS INCURABLY OPPOSED TO THE INTERESTS OF HUMANITY.

I have endeavoured in the preceding pages to point out all the different modes in which natural religion acts injuriously upon the temporal happiness of society. One species of injury yet remains to be indicated, and that too of incalculable effect and permanence—partly as it is productive of distinct mischief, independently and on its own account—partly as it subsidizes a standing army for the perpetuation of all the rest.

Those, who believe in the existence and earthly agency of a superhuman being, view all facts which they are unable to interpret, as special interventions of the celestial hand. Incomprehensible phenomena are ascribed naturally to the incomprehensible person above. They call forth of course the deepest horror and astonishment, as being sudden eruptions of the super-aërial volcano, and reminding the spectator of its unsubdued and inexhaustible terrors. When any such events take place, therefore, his mind is extremely embarrassed and unhinged, and in the highest degree unfit for measuring the correctness of any inferences which immediate fear may suggest.

Now incomprehensible phenomena occur very frequently in the persons of different men—that is, certain men are often seen to act in a manner which the spectator is unable to reconcile with the general principles of human action, so far as they are known to him. Incomprehensible men and incomprehensible modes of behaviour, when they do thus happen, are of course subject to the same construction as other unintelligible events, and are supposed to indicate a signal interference of the Deity. When therefore the actions of any man differ strikingly from the ordinary march of human conduct, we naturally imagine him to be under the peculiar impulse and guidance of the divine finger.

Of incomprehensible behaviour the two extremes, though diametrically opposite kinds, are superior wisdom, and extravagant folly. A loftier and better cultivated intelligence attains his ends by means which we cannot fathom—overleaps difficulties which seem to us insurmountable—foresees consequences which we had never dreamt of. His system of action is to us altogether perplexing and inexplicable. There are others again who seem insensible to the ordinary motives of man—whose thoughts, words, and deeds are alike incoherent and inconsequential—whose incapacity disqualifies them from the commonest offices of life. Such is the other species of incomprehensible man, whom we generally term an idiot or madman, according to circumstances. Both the extremes of intelligence and folly thus exhibit phenomena which we are unable to account for, and are each therefore referred to the immediate influence and inspiration of God.[5]

Amongst early societies, where a very limited number of phenomena have yet been treasured up for comparison, and where the established general principles are built upon so narrow an induction, events are perpetually occurring which seem at variance with them. The sum of principles thus established is called *the course of nature* and the exceptions to them, or supernatural inroads, are extremely frequent. Accordingly, men of unaccountable powers and behaviour are easy to be found, where the standard of comparison is so imperfectly known; and the belief in particular persons, as inspired by God, is proportionably prevalent in an early stage of society.

Conformably to the foregoing doctrine, we find that rude nations generally consider madmen and idiots as persons under the impulse of unseen spirits, and view them with peculiar awe and rev-

---

5. In a former part of this volume, I have assimilated the God of natural religion, on the ground of his attribute of incomprehensibility, to a madman. But as this property is here asserted to belong to the superior intelligence also, it may be asked why I did not compare the divine being to him, instead of choosing a simile apparently so inappropriate. In reply to this, I must introduce a concise but satisfactory distinction.

The madman is one, incomprehensible both in the ends which he seeks and in the means which he takes to attain them—one whose desires and schemes are alike inconsistent and unfathomable. The superior genius is one, whose ends we can understand and assign perfectly, but whose means for attaining them are inexplicable—inasmuch as his fertility of invention, and originality of thought, has enabled him to combine his operations in a manner never previously witnessed.

Now both the ends which the Deity proposes, and the means by which he pursues them, are alike above the comprehension of our finite intellects. And this suffices to vindicate the propriety of my original comparison.

erence. This however, though a remarkable fact and signally illustrative of the principle, yet leads to no important consequences and may be dismissed without farther comment. But the belief of a divine inspiration and concomitancy in persons of superior intelligence, is productive of great and lasting changes in the structure of the social union; and it is most instructive as well as curious to trace the gradual progress of these alterations. A madman is unable to take advantage of any prejudice existing in his favour among mankind, or to push such a feeling into its most profitable result. It terminates, therefore, in those spontaneous effusions of reverence, which do not extend their effects beyond the actual moment and individual.

In order to lead to any lasting consequence, it is necessary that the performer of incomprehensible acts should possess sufficient acuteness to take advantage of the inference which mankind are disposed to draw from them. He need not indeed be a first-rate intellect—but he must be some degrees above a madman or an idiot.

The inferences which an unenlightened mind is in this case inclined to adopt, are indeed most extensive and important. A man is seen, or believed, to produce some given effect, by means which the spectators did not before know to be adequate to that effect: Astonished at such an unforeseen result, they think they cannot too highly magnify the extent of his power. It has already surpassed their anticipations very much—therefore there is no knowing by how much more it may surpass them—no possibility of conceiving its limits. He is therefore invested for the time with omnipotence, by the supposed momentary descent and co-operation of the unseen Being above. But if the Almighty has condescended to pay such pointed attention to any individual, this must be owing to some very peculiar intimacy between them. The individual must possess extraordinary means of recommending himself to the favour of God, in order to attract the distinction of a supernatural visit, and to be honoured with the temporary loan of a fraction of omnipotence. He must stand high in the estimation of the Deity, and must therefore be well acquainted with his disposition, and with the modes of conciliating or provoking him.

Such are the long train of inferences which the performance of an unaccountable act suggests to the alarmed beholders. It is important to remark the gigantic strides by which the mind is hurried on it knows not where, beyond all power of stoppage or limit, the moment it quits the guidance of observation, and is induced to harbour *extra-experimental* belief. A man is seen to do an incomprehensible deed: The utmost consequence which experience would extract from this, would be, that under circumstances not very dissimilar, the same man could repeat the deed. If a king is seen to remove one man's scrofula by the touch, experience might warrant us in conjecturing, that he might cure the same disease in another: But it would be as ridiculous to infer from this single fact, that he possessed the power of performing any other feats, as it would be to conclude that, because mercury quickened the action of the liver, you might rely upon it for the alleviation of the gout. Such, I say, would be the conclusion of a rational observer. But the mind, when once disengaged from observation, and initiated into extra-experimental belief, rolls about without measure in her newly acquired phrenzy, and glances in a moment from earth to heaven and from heaven to earth. To him that hath, more shall be given: Pursuant to this maxim, we ascribe to the man who astonishes us by one incomprehensible feat, the ability of astonishing us still more by a great many others. Nay, the power, which we are led to conceive as exerted, seems too vast to be ascribed to him alone. We therefore introduce an omnipotent accomplice into the scene, and regard the feat as indicating the intervention of a hand sufficiently mighty to work any imaginable marvel. Such is the prompt and forcible transit whereby the *extra-experimental* believer is hurried on to swell the power which he beholds into a greater, and that still farther into the greatest—until at last an act of legerdemain is magnified into an exhibition of omnipotence.

But however unwarranted the inferences thus stated may appear, their effect is not the less important. The wonder-worker gains credit for possessing an extent of power to which we can assign no limits; We view him as a privileged being, possessed of a general power of attorney from the Almighty to interpret his feelings, to promulgate his will, and to draw for supernatural recompense and punishments at pleasure. In virtue of this extensive deputation, the principal becomes responsible for every thing which his emissary says and does, and is supposed to resign the whole management of earthly affairs in favour of the latter.

A wonder-worker thus, by merely producing an adequate measure of astonishment in the bosoms of mankind, is immediately exalted into a station of supreme necessity and importance. All knowledge of the divine will, all assistance from the divine power, can only be attained through his mediation. The patronage thus ascribed to him is enormous, and is, like all other patronage, readily convertible into every other sort of emolument or desirable object. Every one who seeks the divine favour, will not fail to propitiate the minister by whom his petition must be countersigned—whose blessing or curse determines his future treatment at the hands of the Deity. Knowledge of the divine intentions is another perennial source of influence and lucre to the wonder-worker. Hence he is supposed to foreknow the phenomena of nature, and the ignorant, when in doubt, regulate their behaviour by the results which he prognosticates. His patent too of interpreting the divine decrees, to which no competitor has any access, virtually empowers him to manufacture a decalogue on his own account, and to enforce its mandates by all the terrors of spiritual police and penalties.

Powers of such tremendous magnitude appear amply sufficient to enslave and lay prostrate the whole community. And this they infallibly would do, were the extra-experimental belief steady, equable, and consistent with itself, always applying similar principles on similar occasions; and if it were never over-borne by the more immediate motives and acquisitions of earth. The urgent necessity of providing for temporal exigencies, which are too pressing to await the result of an application to heaven, impels the minds of men in another direction, and models their associations more and more according to the dictates of experience. Having acquired, by their own exertions, the means of satisfying their wants, they have not so great an occasion for aërial aid, and all successive accumulations of knowledge tend to weaken the influence of the divine deputy over them.

My present purpose, however, is to investigate not so much the extent of this influence, as the direction in which it operates. We design to shew, that the performer of prodigies (or this class, if there be more than one) when elevated to the post of interpreter and administrator of the divine will, and exercising an influence built upon these privileges—becomes animated with an interest incurably and in every point hostile to human happiness: That their sway can only be matured and perfected by the entire abasement and dismantling of the human faculties; and that therefore all their energies must be devoted to the accomplishment of this destructive work, by the best means which opportunity presents.

1. They have the strongest interest in the depravation of the human intellect. For the demand for their services as agents for the temporal aid of the Deity, altogether depends upon human ignorance and incapacity, and is exactly proportional to it. Why does a man apply for the divine assistance? Because he does not know how to accomplish his ends without it, or how to procure the requisite apparatus for the purpose. If he knew any physical means of attaining it, he would unquestionably prefer them. Every extension therefore of physical methods in the gratification of our wishes,

displaces and throws out of employment by so much the labour of the aërial functionaries. No one prays for the removal of a disease by supernatural aid, when he once knows an appropriate surgical remedy. He therefore who lives by the commission which he charges on the disposal of the former, has a manifest interest in checking the advance and introduction of the latter.

Besides, the accumulation of experimental knowledge excludes the supernatural man from another of his most lucrative employments—that of predicting future events. Those who are the most ignorant of physical connections, and therefore the least qualified to form a judgment as to any particular result, are of course the most frequent in their applications for extra-physical guidance, and the most likely to follow it. This is their sole mode of procuring the most indispensable of all acquisitions. Upon them too it is the most easy to palm a vague and oracular response or decree as to the future, capable of applying to almost any result; And they are the most easily imposed upon by shifts and pretences which veil the incapacity of the respondent. When mankind advance a little in knowledge, and become inquisite, the task of the soothsayer becomes more and more difficult; whereas ignorance and credulity are duped without any great pains. The supernatural agent therefore has a deadly interest against the advance of knowledge, not only as it introduces a better machinery for obtaining acquaintance with the future, and thereby throws him out of employment as a prophet—but also as it enables mankind to detect the hollow, fictitious, and illusory nature of his own predicting establishment.

2. As he is interested in impeding the progress of knowledge, so he is not the less interested in propagating and cherishing *extra-experimental* belief. Ignorance is his negative ally, cutting off mankind from any other means of satisfying their wants except those which he alone can furnish: *Extra-experimental* belief is the

substratum on which all his influence is built. It is this which furnishes to mankind all their evidence of the being, a power and agency of his invisible principal, and also of the posthumous scenes in preparation for us, where these are to be exhibited on a superior and perfect scale. It is this too which supplies mankind with the credentials of his own missions, and makes them impute to him at once, and without cavilling, all that long stretch of aërial dignity and prerogative, the actual proof of which it would have been difficult for him to have gone through. Both the hopes and fears, therefore, which call for his interference, and the selection of him as the person to remove them, rest upon the maintenance of extra-experimental persuasion in the human breast. Were belief closely and inseparably knit with experience, he would never obtain credit for the power of doing any thing else than what mankind really saw him do. His interest accordingly prompts him to disjoin the two—to disjoin them on *every* occasion in his power, if he would ensure their disjunction for his own particular case.

Any one therefore whose power and credit with mankind, rest upon the imputation of supernatural ambassadorship, must be impelled by the most irresistible motives to disunite belief from experience in the bosoms of mankind, as much as he possibly can.

3. Take the same person again, in his capacity of licensed interpreter of the divine will and decrees. What edicts will he be likely to promulgate, as emanating from this consecrated source?

The only circumstance which makes the power of the law-interpreter inferior to that of the legislator, is the accessibility of the text which he professes to explain. Where this is open to the whole public as well as to him, his explanation may be controverted, and recourse will then be had to the production of the original. But if either there exist no original at all, or the interpreter possesses the exclusive custody of it, his power is completely equivalent to that of a legislator.

Now in one of these two alternatives stand the divine decrees. Either there never were any original decrees at all—or if there were, they have been deposited in a spot unknown to any one except the authorised interpreters. And therefore the latter become in fact legislators, issuing whatever edicts they choose in the name and on the behalf of their invisible master—and enforcing them ad libitum by any imaginable measure of punishment or reward, drawn from his inexhaustible magazines.

Now what principle will govern the enactments of an interpreter, or licensed class of interpreters, when thus exercising an unfettered power of legislation? The general principles of human nature suffer us not to hesitate a moment in answering this question. It will be a regard to their own separate interest. Like all other monopolists who possess the exclusive privilege of rendering any particular service—like all other possessors of power independent of, and irresponsible to, the community—they will pursue the natural path of self-preference, and will apply their functions to purposes of aggrandizement and exaction.

Now this separate interest is irreconcileably at variance with that of the society. If any man, or any separate class, are permitted to legislate for their own benefit, they are in effect despots; while the rest of the community are degraded to the level of slaves, and will be treated as such by the legislative system so constructed. Conformable to this system the precepts delivered by the supernatural delegate as enacted by his invisible master, will be such as to subjugate the minds of the community, in the highest practicable degree, to himself and to his brethren, and to appropriate for the benefit of the class as much wealth and power as circumstances will permit. This is a mere statement of the dictates of self-preference.

4. To effect this purpose, he will find it essentially necessary to describe the Deity as capricious, irritable, and vindictive, to the

highest extent—as regarding with gloom and jealousy the enjoyments of the human worm, and taking delight in his privations or sufferings—pliable indeed without measure, and yielding up instantaneously all his previous sentiments, when technically and professionally solicited—but requiring the perpetual application of emolients to sooth his wrathful propensities. The more implicitly mankind believe in these appalling attributes, the more essential is he who can stand in the gap and avert the threatened pestilence—the more necessary is it to ensure his activity by feeling and ennobling him. On whatever occasions he can, in the capacity of interpreter to the divine will, persuade them that they are exposed to supernatural wrath—in all such junctures, he will obtain a fee, as mediator or intercessor, for procuring a reprieve.

The more therefore he can multiply the number of offences against God, the greater does his profit become—because on every such act of guilt, the sinner will find it answer to forestall the execution of the sentence by effecting an amicable compromise with the vicegerent of the Almighty. For rendering so important a service, the latter may make his own terms.

But in order to multiply offences, the most efficacious method is to prohibit those acts which there is the most frequent and powerful temptation to commit. Now the temptation to perform any act is of course proportional to the magnitude of the pleasurable, and the smallness of the painful, consequences by which it is attended. Those deeds, therefore, which are the most delightful, and the most innoxious, will meet with the severest prohibitions in the religious code, and be represented as the most deeply offensive to the divine majesty. Because such deeds will be most frequently repeated and will accordingly create the amplest demand for the expiatory formula.

Such therefore will be the code constructed by the supernatural delegate in the name of his unearthly sovereign—including the most rigorous denunciations against human pleasure, and interdicting it the more severly in proporation as it is delicious and harmless. He will enjoin the most gratuitous and unrequited privations, and self-imposed sufferings, as the sole method of conciliating the divine mercy,—inasmuch as the neglect of these mandates must be the most common, and all such remissness will incur a penalty which the transgressor must be compelled to redeem.

5. All the purchase which the interpreter of the divine will has upon the human mind, depends upon the extent of its superhuman apprehensions. It is therefore his decided interest that the dread of these unseen visitations should haunt the bosoms of mankind, like a heavy and perpetual incubus, day and night—that they should live under a constant sense of the suspended arm of God—and thus in a state of such conscious insecurity and helplessness, that all possibility of earthly comfort should be altogether blighted and cast out. The more firmly these undefined terrors can be planted in a man's associations, the more urgent is his need of a mediator with the aërial kingdom to which his apprehensions refer, and the more enormous the sacrifices which he will make in order to purchase such intercession.

6. Again, it will be the decided interest of the inspired legislator, to clothe all his enactments in the most imposing epithets of moral approbation—to describe the Being, by whom he is commissioned, in terms which imply the holiest and most beneficent character, though the proceedings and the system which he attributes to him indicate the very opposite temper—and to make mankind believe that every act of this Being is, and must be, just. By thus perverting their moral sentiments, he tightens and perpetuates the pressure of superhuman apprehensions. There will be less tendency to murmur and revolt at these threats, when men are persuaded that they have justly incurred the anger of an all-beneficent Being.

By this analysis, I think, it appears most demonstratively, that all those whose influence rests on an imputed connexion with the Divine Being, cannot fail to be animated by an interest incurably opposed to all human happiness: that the inevitable aim of such persons must be to extend and render irremediable, those evils which natural religion would originate without them, viz, ignorance, extra-experimental belief, appalling conceptions of the Deity, intense dread of his visitations, and a perversion of the terms of praise and censure in his behalf. To this identity of result I have traced them both, although by different and perfectly unconnected roads.

Natural religion is thus provided with an array of human force and fraud for the purpose of enforcing her mandates, and realising her mischievous tendencies. A standing army of ministers is organized in her cause, formed either of men who are themselves believed to be specially gifted from the sky, or of others who pretend not to any immediate inspiration in their own persons, but merely act as the sub-delegates of some heaven-commissioned envoy of aforetime. The interest of both these sorts of persons is precisely identical, nor is it of the smallest importance whether the patent is worked by the original pretender, or by any one else into whose hands it may have subsequently fallen. In either case its fruits are equally deleterious.

In either case, the same conspirators league themselves for the same purposes—that of promulgating and explaining the will of their incomprehensible master, and subjugating to his thraldom the knowledge and the hopes of mankind. And the accession of strength, which religion derives from this special confederation in her favour, is incalculable. They supply many defects, in her means of conquest and influence, which must otherwise have rendered her dominion comparatively narrow.

First, one grand deficiency in unofficered religion, is the

absence of any directive rule. Mankind, from their conceptions of the character of the Deity, will doubtless conjecture what sort of conduct will be agreeable to him, and will also fix upon some particular actions belonging to that course as more agreeable than others. But this unguided and promiscuous selection is not likely to be either uniform, earnest, or circumstantial.

When a body of authorised agents is framed, through whom the designs and temper of the Deity can be learnt, this defect is completely supplied. The ceremonial pleasing to him is then officially declared: the acts offensive to him are enumerated and defined, and their greater or less enormity graduated. Doubt and controversy are precluded, or at least exceedingly narrowed, by an appeal to the recognized organ of infallibility. And thus the superhuman terrors are concentrated and particularized, whereby they are brought to act in the most cogent and effective manner which the nature of the case admits.

2. In analysing the efficiency of the religious sanctions, we have already seen that their remoteness and uncertainty will not allow of their producing a steady, equable and unvarying impression upon the mind—although at peculiar moments, these apprehensions become supreme and overwhelming, even to insanity. For motives thus subject to fluctuation, the constant presence of a standing brotherhood is peculiarly requisite, in order to watch those periods when the mind is most vulnerable to their influence—to multiply and perpetuate, if possible, these temporary liabilities, and to secure the production of some permanent result during the continuance of the fit. The ministers of natural religion, by bringing their most efficient batteries to bear upon the mind at these intervals, frequently succeed in extending the duration of the supernatural fears, and subjugating the whole man for life.

Sickness—mental affliction—approaching death—childhood—all these are periods when the intellect is depressed and feeble, and when the associations are peculiarly liable to the inroads of every species of fear. They are times therefore when the officer of the invisible world exercises the most uncontrolled despotism over the soul, and bends it whither he will. Were it not for his dexterity in contriving to render the bias permanent, the sick or the despondent would probably relapse, in no long period, into their habitual state, of comparative insensibility to supernatural terrors.

With regard to the dying man, indeed, no ulterior views can be entertained; but the immediate effect of the presence and ascendancy of a religious minister, on this occasion is most important. Without his aid, posthumous apprehensions would indeed embitter the hour of death, but this would be productive of no subsequent evil. The minister not only aggravates these terrors to an infinitely higher pitch, but offers to the distracted patient a definite and easy mode by which he may in part alleviate them, and lessen the impending risk. He must make some atonement or satisfaction to God, in return for the offensive acts with which his life has abounded, by transferring a part of the whole of that property which he is at all events about to leave behind. But as he cannot have access in person to the offended principal, this property must be handed over in trust to his accredited agent or minister, for the inaccessible party. By such testamentary donation the sins of the past are in part redeemed.

The religious fears attending upon the hour of death are thus converted into powerful engines for enriching the sacerdotal class, who contrive to extract this lasting profit from an affection of mind which would otherwise have caused nothing beyond momentary pain. The act of mortmain attests the height to which these death-bed commutations have actually been carried: Nor is it extravagant to assert, that had there been no change of the public sentiment and no interposition of the legislature, nearly all the land of England would have become the property of the church.

3. It should by no means be forgotten, that the inefficiency, and the alternation from general indifference to occasional fever, which I have shewn to belong to the religious sanction, constitute the leading source of importance and emolument to the priesthood. Suppose mankind to be perfectly acquainted with all the modifications of the Divine temper, and strictly observant of his commands, the functions of this class would of course become extinct. There would be no necessity for their services either as interpreters, mediators, or intercessors.

It is their decisive interest to multiply offences, as preparations for the lucrative season of repentance, during which their sway is at its zenith, and their most advantageous contracts realized. For each crime a pardon must be obtained through the intercession and agency of the authorized mediator. He must therefore be propitiated by payment both in money and honour, and the profits of the sacerdotal body bear an accurate ratio to the number of offences committed, and of pardons implored.

Thus the nature of the religious sanction, though very ill adapted for the purpose of actually terminating the practices it forbids, is yet calculated in the most precise manner to exalt and enrich the officers busied in enforcing it. This is the end, at which, supposing them like other men, they will be constantly aiming, and they have enjoyed facilities in the attainment of it rarely possessed by mere intermediate agents.

For, first, they have found posthumous terror, from its instability and occasional fierceness, an exquisite preparative of the mind for their dominion. And, secondly, they have united two functions which have placed this feeling entirely under their direction—They are, ex-officio, both framers of the divine law, and venders of the divine pardons for infringements of it. They have named the acts which required forgiveness as well as the price at which forgiveness should be purchased. Suppose only the periodical spring-tides of superhuman fear to reach a certain height, and this machinery for subjugation becomes perfect and irresistible.

If in earthly matters, these two functions were united—if the same person were to become framer of the law, and agent for the sale of licences to elude it—it is manifest, that he would make terrestrial laws inconceivably burdensome and exactive, so that there should be no possibility of observing them. The interest of the sacerdotal class has been completely similar, leading them to require, in the name of the Deity, obedience where obedience is impracticable, and then making men pay for the deficiency. Accordingly they inform us that he is a Being of such an exquisite and irritable temperament—so nicely susceptible and so vehemently impatient of every thing which is not exactly like himself, that we cannot escape his displeasure, except by undergoing a thorough repair and regeneration upon the celestial model. If but the most transient wish for any thing unlike to God, or unholy, shoots across the mind, it constitutes criminality and is deeply abhorrent to the divine perfection. To such a state of entire conformity no human being ever yet attained—and thus, by the invention of an impracticable code, mankind are placed in a constant necessity of discharging expiatory fees, and purchasing licences of evasion.

In this respect, the sacerdotal interest is directly at variance not only with that of the human race, but also with that of the divine Being. He sincerely desires, without doubt, that his edicts should be strictly obeyed, and therefore would be willing to facilitate their excecution, so far as is consistent with his own sensitive and exquisite purity. But the middlemen who pretend to serve him have unfortunately an interest in their non-performance, and therefore throw every possible obstacle in the way of obedience.

4. In a former part of this work, I endeavoured to shew, that the real actuating force which gave birth to religious deeds, though so masked as not to be discernible on a superficial view, was *public*

opinion. There cannot be a more effectual spur to this popular sentiment, than the formation of a body whose peculiar interest lies in watching its various turns, in kindling it anew, and dexterously diversifying its applications. For this task they possess numerous advantages. The necessity of recurring to their services on many occasions ensures to them a large measure of respect, as well as of wealth, and this re-acts upon the function which they exercise. They labour sedulously to inculcate the deepest reverence in speaking of religious matters, as well as extreme backwardness and timidity of soul in subjecting them to the examination of reason. They diffuse widely among the community those pious misapplications of moral epithets, which are inseparably annexed to the natural belief in an omnipotent Being, availing themselves of this confusion of language to stigmatize as iniquitous every thing which counteracts their own views, and to extol as virtuous that which favours them.

By thus whipping up and propagating the religious antipathies of mankind, they generally succeed in organizing that tone of public opinion which is most conducive to their interest: That is, a sentiment which rigorously enforces a certain measure of religious observance—while it also recognizes in words, as incumbent and necessary duties of piety, a number of other acts which no one ever performs, and which mankind will allow you to leave undone, provided you do not question the propriety of doing them. A variance is thus introduced between the religious feelings and the reigning practice, and whenever any accident preternaturally kindles the former, such a laxity of conduct will of course appear pregnant with guilt. Hence that ebb and flow of mind, and those periodical spasms of repentant alarm, which can only be charmed away by purchasing comfort at the hands of the spiritual exorcist. And thus the constitution of the public sentiment becomes a preparation and medium for the effectual dominion of this class.

5. The fundamental principle, upon which all the superhuman machinery rests its hold, has been shewn to consist in *extra-experimental* belief. Now in diffusing and strengthening this species of persuasion, the sacerdotal body form most essential auxiliaries. They are the legitimate and acknowledged interpreters of all incomprehensible events, and any inference which they extract from thence is universally adopted. This bestows upon them an unlimited licence of coining and circulating as much *extra-experimental* matter as they choose, and of distorting the physical links among phenomena by smuggling in an appeal to the divine intentions. By their constant and well-paid activity, also, every casual coincidence is magnified into a prodigy—every prediction accidentally verified, into a proof of their free-right of admission behind the unexpanded scenes of futurity. Besides, they are continually at hand to spread abroad those myriads of fictions, which the *extra-experimental* belief has been shewn to engender. Mendacity itself becomes consecrated, when employed in behalf of religion; and the infinity of pious frauds, which may be cited from the pages of history, sufficiently attests the zeal and effect with which the sacerdotal class have laboured in the diffusion of this unreal currency.

From this successive accumulation of particular instances, a large aggregate of *extra-experimental* matter is at last amassed, which lays claim to the title and honours or a separate science. The stories upon which it is founded are so thickly and authoritatively spread abroad—apparently so unconnected one with the other, and relying upon numerous separate attestations—that it seems impossible to discredit the whole, and difficult to know where to draw the line. To fulfil so nice a task, writers arise who compare the different stories together, arrange them into a systematic order, extract meaning and inferences from these collations, and reject those particulars which cannot be reconciled with the theories thus elicited. This aërial matter is distributed into a regular and distinct branch of knowledge, partitioned into various subordinate departments, and the sacerdotal class of course monopolize the guidance and guardianship of this science almost exclusively to themselves. We have only to consult the first book of *Cicero de Divinatione*, in order to observe the minute subdivisions which the imaginary science of augury underwent in those times—the formal array of conclusions which appear to be strictly deduced from its alleged facts, and the various philosophical systems framed to explain and reconcile them.

Accordingly the *extra-experimental* belief, when sufficiently augmented in volume, becomes possessed of a distinct station among the sciences, and reflects upon its practitioners and professors all that credit which is annexed to superiority in any other department. Realities become divided into two separate classes: First, the world of experience, embracing all which we see, feel, hear, taste, or smell, and the various connections among them. Secondly, the world of which we have no experience, consisting of what are called immaterial entities, or of those things which we neither see, nor feel, nor hear, nor taste, nor smell; but which, nevertheless, we are supposed to know without any experience at all. The latter science is always the colleague and correlative of the former—frequently indeed it is more highly esteemed and more assiduously cultivated.

I have endeavoured to trace some of those modes, in which the brotherhood hired and equipped by natural religion have contrived to promote, in so high a degree, the success of the cause inscribed on their banners—and in so much higher a degree, to aggrandize and enrich themselves. My sketch, indeed, has been exceedingly superficial and incomplete; because the facilities which such a standing corps possesses for compassing its ends, are both innumerable and indescribable. We ought not however to forget, that a wealthy and powerful body of this kind not only acts with its own force, but also with that of all who have anything to hope, or to fear, from it. To become a member of the body constitutes a valuable object of ambition, and all, who have any chance of attaining such a post, will of course conspire vehemently in its support. Besides, there arises a long train of connections and dependants, who diffuse themselves every where through the community, and contribute most materially to spread and enhance the influence of the class.

In addition to these, however, they have yet another ally, more powerful and efficient than all the rest,—the earthly chief, or governing power of the state. He, as well as they, has an interest incurably at variance with that of the community, and all sinister interests have a natural tendency to combine together and to co-operate, inasmuch as the object of each is thereby most completely and most easily secured. But between the particular interest of a governing aristocracy and a sacerdotal class, there seems a very peculiar affinity and coincidence—each wielding the precise engine which the other wants.

The aristocracy, for instance, possess the disposal of a mass of physical force sufficient to crush any partial resistance, and demand only to be secured against any very general or simultaneous opposition on the part of the community. To make this sure, they are obliged to maintain a strong purchase upon the public mind, and to chain it down to the level of submission—to plant within it feelings which may neutralize all hatred of slavery, and facilitate the business of spoliation. For this purpose the sacerdotal class are most precisely and most happily cut out. By their influence over the moral sentiments, they place implicit submission among the first of all human duties. They infuse the deepest reverence for temporal power, by considering the existing authorities as established and consecrated by the immaterial Autocrat above, and as identified with his divine majesty. The duty of mankind towards the earthly government becomes thus the same as duty to God—that is, an unvarying "prostration both of the understanding and will." Besides this direct debasement of the moral faculties for the purpose of assuring non-resistance, the supernatural terrors, and the *extra-experimental* belief, which the priest-hood are so industrious in diffusing, all tend to the very same result. They produce that mistrust, alarm, and insecurity, which disposes a man to bless himself in any little fragment of present enjoyment, while it stifles all aspirations for future improvement and even all ideas of its practicability.

Such is the tacit and surreptitious, though incessant and effectual, operation on the public sentiment, by which the priest-hood keep down all disposition on the part of mankind to oppose the inroads of their governors. Their influence is perhaps greater when they preach thus on behalf of the government, than on their own. Because in the former case, the interest which they have in the doctrine is not so obvious, and they appear like impartial counsellors, inculcating a behaviour of which they themselves are first to set the example.

The earthly ruler, on the other hand, amply repays the co-operation which he has thus derived. The mental (or psychagogical) machinery of the priest-hood is very excellent; but they are unhappily dificient in physical force. Hence the protection of the earthly potentate is of most essential utility to a class so defectively provided in this main point. The coercion which he supplies is all sanctified by the holy name of religion, in defence of which it is resorted to; and he is extolled, while thus engaged, as the disinterested servant of the invisible Being. He is therefore permitted to employ, in behalf of religion, an extent and disposition of force which would have provoked indignation and revolt, on any other account.

The utmost extent of physical force, which circumstances will permit, is in this manner put forward, to smother any symptom of impiety, or even of dissent from the sacerdotal dogmas: Irreligion and heresy become crimes of the deepest dye, and the class are thus secured, in their task of working on the public mind, from all competition or contest. Under the protection of such powerful artillery, this corps of sappers and miners carries on a tranquil, but effectual, progress in the trenches.

Nor is it merely a negative aid which the earthly governor extends to them. He extorts from the people, in their favour, a large compulsory tribute, in order to maintain them in affluence and in worldly credit; thus securing to them an additional purchase upon the public sentiment, and confirming his own safety from resistance. Under no other pretence could he induce the people to pay taxes, specially for the purpose of quartering throughout the country a standing army of advocates to check and counteract all opinions unfavourable to himself. They may be brought to this sacrifice in behalf of a sacerdotal class, whose interest, by the forced provision thus obtained, becomes still more closely identified with that of the earthly ruler.

One of the most noxious properties therefore, in the profession of men to which natural religion gives birth, is its coincidence and league with the sinister interests of earth—a coincidence so entire, as to secure unity of design on the part of both, without any necessity for special confederation, and therefore more mischievously efficient than it would have proved had the deed of partnership been open and proclaimed. Prostration and plunder of the community is indeed the common end of both. The only point upon which there can be any dissension, is about the partition of the spoil—and quarrels of this nature have occasionally taken place, in cases where the passive state of the people has obviated all apprehension of resistance. In general, however, the necessity of strict amity has been too visible to admit of much discord, and the division of the spoil has been carried on tranquilly, though in different ratios, according to the tone of the public mind.

GREAT BOOKS IN PHILOSOPHY PAPERBACK SERIES

ESTHETICS

- ❑ Aristotle—*The Poetics*
- ❑ Aristotle—*Treatise on Rhetoric*

ETHICS

- ❑ Aristotle—*The Nicomachean Ethics*
- ❑ Marcus Aurelius—*Meditations*
- ❑ Jeremy Bentham—*The Principles of Morals and Legislation*
- ❑ John Dewey—*Human Nature and Conduct*
- ❑ John Dewey—*The Moral Writings of John Dewey, Revised Edition* (edited by James Gouinlock)
- ❑ Epictetus—*Enchiridion*
- ❑ Immanuel Kant—*Fundamental Principles of the Metaphysic of Morals*
- ❑ John Stuart Mill—*Utilitarianism*
- ❑ George Edward Moore—*Principia Ethica*
- ❑ Friedrich Nietzsche—*Beyond Good and Evil*
- ❑ Plato—*Protagoras*, *Philebus*, and *Gorgias*
- ❑ Bertrand Russell—*Bertrand Russell On Ethics, Sex, and Marriage* (edited by Al Seckel)
- ❑ Arthur Schopenhauer—*The Wisdom of Life* and *Counsels and Maxims*
- ❑ Adam Smith—*The Theory of Moral Sentiments*
- ❑ Benedict de Spinoza—*Ethics* and *The Improvement of the Understanding*

METAPHYSICS/EPISTEMOLOGY

- ❑ Aristotle—*De Anima*
- ❑ Aristotle—*The Metaphysics*
- ❑ Francis Bacon—*Essays*
- ❑ George Berkeley—*Three Dialogues Between Hylas and Philonous*
- ❑ W. K. Clifford—*The Ethics of Belief and Other Essays* (introduction by Timothy J. Madigan)
- ❑ René Descartes—*Discourse on Method* and *The Meditations*
- ❑ John Dewey—*How We Think*
- ❑ John Dewey—*The Influence of Darwin on Philosophy and Other Essays*
- ❑ Epicurus—*The Essential Epicurus: Letters, Principal Doctrines, Vatican Sayings, and Fragments* (translated, and with an introduction, by Eugene O'Connor)
- ❑ Sidney Hook—*The Quest for Being*
- ❑ David Hume—*An Enquiry Concerning Human Understanding*
- ❑ David Hume—*Treatise of Human Nature*

- ❑ William James—*The Meaning of Truth*
- ❑ William James—*Pragmatism*
- ❑ Immanuel Kant—*The Critique of Judgment*
- ❑ Immanuel Kant—*Critique of Practical Reason*
- ❑ Immanuel Kant—*Critique of Pure Reason*
- ❑ Gottfried Wilhelm Leibniz—*Discourse on Metaphysics* and the *Monadology*
- ❑ John Locke—*An Essay Concerning Human Understanding*
- ❑ George Herbert Mead—*The Philosophy of the Present*
- ❑ Charles S. Peirce—*The Essential Writings* (edited by Edward C. Moore, preface by Richard Robin)
- ❑ Plato—*The Euthyphro*, *Apology*, *Crito*, and *Phaedo*
- ❑ Plato—*Lysis*, *Phaedrus*, and *Symposium*
- ❑ Bertrand Russell—*The Problems of Philosophy*
- ❑ George Santayana—*The Life of Reason*
- ❑ Sextus Empiricus—*Outlines of Pyrrhonism*
- ❑ Ludwig Wittgenstein—*Wittgenstein's Lectures: Cambridge, 1932–1935* (edited by Alice Ambrose)

PHILOSOPHY OF RELIGION

- ❑ Jeremy Bentham—*The Influence of Natural Religion on the Temporal Happiness of Mankind*
- ❑ Marcus Tullius Cicero—*The Nature of the Gods* and *On Divination*
- ❑ Ludwig Feuerbach—*The Essence of Christianity*
- ❑ David Hume—*Dialogues Concerning Natural Religion*
- ❑ William James—*The Varieties of Religious Experience*
- ❑ John Locke—*A Letter Concerning Toleration*
- ❑ Lucretius—*On the Nature of Things*
- ❑ John Stuart Mill—*Three Essays on Religion*
- ❑ Friedrich Nietzsche—*The Antichrist*
- ❑ Thomas Paine—*The Age of Reason*
- ❑ Bertrand Russell—*Bertrand Russell On God and Religion* (edited by Al Seckel)

SOCIAL AND POLITICAL PHILOSOPHY

- ❑ Aristotle—*The Politics*
- ❑ Mikhail Bakunin—*The Basic Bakunin: Writings, 1869–1871* (translated and edited by Robert M. Cutler)
- ❑ Edmund Burke—*Reflections on the Revolution in France*
- ❑ John Dewey—*Freedom and Culture*
- ❑ John Dewey—*Individualism Old and New*
- ❑ John Dewey—*Liberalism and Social Action*

- ❑ G. W. F. Hegel—*The Philosophy of History*
- ❑ G. W. F. Hegel—*Philosophy of Right*
- ❑ Thomas Hobbes—*The Leviathan*
- ❑ Sidney Hook—*Paradoxes of Freedom*
- ❑ Sidney Hook—*Reason, Social Myths, and Democracy*
- ❑ John Locke—*Second Treatise on Civil Government*
- ❑ Niccolo Machiavelli—*The Prince*
- ❑ Karl Marx (with Friedrich Engels)—*The German Ideology*, including *Theses on Feuerbach and Introduction to the Critique of Political Economy*
- ❑ Karl Marx—*The Poverty of Philosophy*
- ❑ Karl Marx/Friedrich Engels—*The Economic and Philosophic Manuscripts of 1844* and *The Communist Manifesto*
- ❑ John Stuart Mill—*Considerations on Representative Government*
- ❑ John Stuart Mill—*On Liberty*
- ❑ John Stuart Mill—*On Socialism*
- ❑ John Stuart Mill—*The Subjection of Women*
- ❑ Montesquieu, Charles de Secondat—*The Spirit of Laws*
- ❑ Friedrich Nietzsche—*Thus Spake Zarathustra*
- ❑ Thomas Paine—*Common Sense*
- ❑ Thomas Paine—*Rights of Man*
- ❑ Plato—*Laws*
- ❑ Plato—*The Republic*
- ❑ Jean-Jacques Rousseau—*The Social Contract*
- ❑ Mary Wollstonecraft—*A Vindication of the Rights of Men*
- ❑ Mary Wollstonecraft—*A Vindication of the Rights of Women*

GREAT MINDS PAPERBACK SERIES

ART

- ❑ Leonardo da Vinci—*A Treatise on Painting*

CRITICAL ESSAYS

- ❑ Desiderius Erasmus—*The Praise of Folly*
- ❑ Jonathan Swift—*A Modest Proposal and Other Satires* (with an introduction by George R. Levine)
- ❑ H. G. Wells—*The Conquest of Time* (with an introduction by Martin Gardner)

ECONOMICS

- ❑ Charlotte Perkins Gilman—*Women and Economics: A Study of the Economic Relation between Women and Men*
- ❑ John Maynard Keynes—*The General Theory of Employment, Interest, and Money*
- ❑ John Maynard Keynes—*A Tract on Monetary Reform*
- ❑ Thomas R. Malthus—*An Essay on the Principle of Population*
- ❑ Alfred Marshall—*Money, Credit, and Commerce*
- ❑ Alfred Marshall—*Principles of Economics*
- ❑ Karl Marx—*Theories of Surplus Value*
- ❑ David Ricardo—*Principles of Political Economy and Taxation*
- ❑ Adam Smith—*Wealth of Nations*
- ❑ Thorstein Veblen—*Theory of the Leisure Class*

HISTORY

- ❑ Edward Gibbon—*On Christianity*
- ❑ Alexander Hamilton, John Jay, and James Madison—*The Federalist*
- ❑ Herodotus—*The History*
- ❑ Thucydides—*History of the Peloponnesian War*
- ❑ Andrew D. White—*A History of the Warfare of Science with Theology in Christendom*

LAW

- ❑ John Austin—*The Province of Jurisprudence Determined*

PSYCHOLOGY

- ❑ Sigmund Freud—*Totem and Taboo*

RELIGION

- ❑ Thomas Henry Huxley—*Agnosticism and Christianity and Other Essays*
- ❑ Ernest Renan—*The Life of Jesus*
- ❑ Upton Sinclair—*The Profits of Religion*
- ❑ Elizabeth Cady Stanton—*The Woman's Bible*
- ❑ Voltaire—*A Treatise on Toleration and Other Essays*

SCIENCE

- ❑ Jacob Bronowski—*The Identity of Man*
- ❑ Nicolaus Copernicus—*On the Revolutions of Heavenly Spheres*
- ❑ Marie Curie—*Radioactive Substances*
- ❑ Charles Darwin—*The Autobiography of Charles Darwin*
- ❑ Charles Darwin—*The Descent of Man*
- ❑ Charles Darwin—*The Origin of Species*
- ❑ Charles Darwin—*The Voyage of the* Beagle
- ❑ Albert Einstein—*Relativity*
- ❑ Michael Faraday—*The Forces of Matter*
- ❑ Galileo Galilei—*Dialogues Concerning Two New Sciences*
- ❑ Ernst Haeckel—*The Riddle of the Universe*
- ❑ William Harvey—*On the Motion of the Heart and Blood in Animals*
- ❑ Werner Heisenberg—*Physics and Philosophy: The Revolution in Modern Science* (introduction by F. S. C. Northrop)
- ❑ Julian Huxley—*Evolutionary Humanism*
- ❑ Edward Jenner—*Vaccination against Smallpox*
- ❑ Johannes Kepler—*Epitome of Copernican Astronomy* and *Harmonies of the World*
- ❑ Charles Mackay—*Extraordinary Popular Delusions and the Madness of Crowds*
- ❑ James Clerk Maxwell—*Matter and Motion*
- ❑ Isaac Newton—*The Principia*
- ❑ Louis Pasteur and Joseph Lister—*Germ Theory and Its Application to Medicine* and *On the Antiseptic Principle of the Practice of Surgery*
- ❑ William Thomson (Lord Kelvin) and Peter Guthrie Tait—*The Elements of Natural Philosophy*
- ❑ Alfred Russel Wallace—*Island Life*

SOCIOLOGY

- ❑ Emile Durkheim—*Ethics and the Sociology of Morals* (translated with an introduction by Robert T. Hall)